CH00587017

John Pritchard was Bishop of Oxford
He was formerly Bishop of Jarrow a
of Canterbury. He has served in p
Taunton, and was Warden of Cranmer
by the author include *The Intercessions Handbook, The Second
Intercessions Handbook, Beginning Again, How to Pray, How to
Explain Your Faith, The Life and Work of a Priest, Living Jesus,
God Lost and Found, Living Faithfully, Ten* and *Something More.*

THE INTERCESSIONS RESOURCE BOOK

JOHN PRITCHARD

First published in Great Britain in 2018

Society for Promoting Christian Knowledge
36 Causton Street
London SW1P 4ST
www.spck.org.uk

The author and publisher have made every effort to ensure that the external
website and email addresses included in this book are correct and up to date
at the time of going to press. The author and publisher are not responsible
for the content, quality or continuing accessibility of the sites.

Unless otherwise noted, Scripture quotations are taken from the New
Revised Standard Version of the Bible, Anglicized Edition, copyright © 1989,
1995 by the Division of Christian Education of the National Council of the
Churches of Christ in the USA. Used by permission. All rights reserved.

British Library Cataloguing-in-Publication Data
A catalogue record for this book is available from the British Library

ISBN 978–0–281–07821–9
eBook ISBN 978–0–281–07822–6

Typeset by Fakenham Prepress Solutions, Fakenham, Norfolk NR21 8NN
First printed in Great Britain by Ashford Colour Press
Subsequently digitally reprinted in Great Britain

eBook by Fakenham Prepress Solutions, Fakenham, Norfolk NR21 8NN

Produced on paper from sustainable forests

For all those Christians
who faithfully lead intercessions
week by week

CONTENTS

A word at the beginning   xi

1 LEADING INTERCESSIONS IN MAINSTREAM WORSHIP 1

2 WHAT ARE WE DOING WHEN WE INTERCEDE?   5

3 THROUGH THE YEAR   9
   (1) January   9
   (2) February   11
   (3) March   13
   (4) April   15
   (5) May   17
   (6) June   19
   (7) July   21
   (8) August   23
   (9) September   25
   (10) October   27
   (11) November   29
   (12) December   31

4 SEASONS AND FESTIVALS   32
   (13) Advent 1   32
   (14) Advent 2   34
   (15) All Saints   36
   (16) Christmas 1   38
   (17) Christmas 2   40
   (18) Epiphany   42
   (19) Lent 1   44
   (20) Lent 2   46
   (21) Palm Sunday   48
   (22) Good Friday 1   50
   (23) Good Friday 2   52
   (24) Easter 1   54
   (25) Easter 2   56

(26) Sundays after Easter 58
(27) Ascension 1 60
(28) Ascension 2 62
(29) Pentecost 1 64
(30) Pentecost 2 66
(31) Trinity Sunday 68

5 SPECIAL SUNDAYS 70
(32) New Year 70
(33) Mothering Sunday 72
(34) Fathers' Day 74
(35) Harvest 76
(36) Remembrance Sunday 78
(37) Bible Sunday 80
(38) Dedication Festival 82

6 THEMES 84
(39) The Church here and everywhere 84
(40) Silence 86
(41) Work 88
(42) Light 90
(43) Friends 92
(44) Relationships 94
(45) Health 96
(46) Wholeness and sickness 98
(47) Death 100
(48) Storm 102
(49) Loss 104
(50) Sport 106
(51) Community 108
(52) Mess 110
(53) Anxiety 112
(54) Environment 114
(55) Prayer 116
(56) Seeds of prayer 118
(57) Children 1 120
(58) Children 2 122

(59) Home   124
(60) Communication   126
(61) Giving/stewardship   128
(62) Faith and doubt   130
(63) Terrorism   132
(64) The world from space   134
(65) Circles   136
(66) Music   138
(67) One particular person   140
(68) The Beatitudes   142
(69) An ordinary Sunday   144
(70) The Lord's Prayer   146

7 INTERCESSIONS IN INFORMAL WORSHIP, SMALL
  GROUPS AND PRAYER STATIONS   148

8 PERSONAL INTERCESSION   160

9 INTERCESSION FOR EXTROVERTS   169

Notes   173
Further resources   174

A WORD AT THE BEGINNING

This is the third book of intercessions that I've foisted on the Church. It's only because of the welcome the previous two have received that I've presumed to write a third. What I hope this shows is not that I have too much time on my hands, still less that I'm some kind of expert, but rather that there's a continuing hunger among Christians to come before God bearing on our hearts the needs of others and the struggles of the wider world.

It's a huge privilege to be able to intercede for others. Think of it. We are always more than welcome in the halls of heaven, bringing with us our love for others and our concern for their well-being. As we are made welcome it seems that God takes and uses our love and concern – perhaps we might even say that God *needs* it, in order to bring about the best possible outcome for the person or situation we're praying for. Privilege indeed.

Consider God's options, if that isn't blasphemous. With nothing yet on the drawing board God could perhaps have decided to act alone in the world – which would contradict the whole idea of creating persons made in the image of God to inhabit 'his' world. Option two could have been to leave things entirely in human hands with God having no further involvement in human history – which is too frightening even to contemplate. Option three, therefore, is a dialogue between heaven and earth, between God and his enormously loved creatures, through which God engages in human affairs. Guess which option God chose.

And so we intercede. But we don't necessarily find it easy to decide on the right words and ideas. And if we're leading intercessions we don't necessarily find it easy to keep the congregation or group engaged and actively praying. We can easily slip into generalizations, repetition, bland use of language and even – dare I say it? – boredom.

So what I'm trying to do here is to offer a variety of ways of praying for others that might begin to remedy those problems. Not all of them will 'work' for you or for your congregation. Moreover, these are only meant to be 'starters' to be adapted to your local context. They're ideas, prompts, a platform for something authentically yours, because these words are very much *my* voice, and my voice will not be your voice. But I hope they will be sufficient to get the creative juices flowing and to make of intercession a joy not only for you but for those praying through your words.

The most important confidence we have, of course, is that God is listening to what's going on in our hearts, beneath our stumbling words. But words are what we've got, and we might as well make them as helpful as we can as we lay our prayers before the God we love and trust.

Thanks must go as ever to my editor Alison Barr for her encouragement both in this and in many other projects, and to my wife Wendy for her patience both with me and with the raw text of this book. And to those who have valued previous books and wanted more – thank you, be blessed as you continue to lead God's people in one of the most exciting and important activities of the Christian life.

John Pritchard

1 LEADING INTERCESSIONS IN MAINSTREAM WORSHIP

It's very good to see so many different people now leading intercessions in most of our churches. The majority of us see it as a privilege to lead the people of God in prayer and one which we take with great seriousness. In preparing the prayers it's worth our while thinking through the following points:

What kind of service is this? Will it have a particular theme from the Church's year or the life of the local church? How formal or informal will the service be? Will it have many children present? Will the service lend itself to more meditative prayers or should they be short and to the point? And, importantly, what theme will the preacher be exploring in the sermon? (An email or quick phone call should unearth that information, but not too early in the week . . .)

How might the congregation be feeling? What's going on in the life of the nation that might be on people's minds and affect their mood? Or what's happening in the life of the local church (a significant bereavement, changes in leadership, a new programme starting)? Does the season of the year affect people's mood? Does this congregation find experiment helpful or not? We have to put ourselves in the mood and minds of the hearers of our prayers, not stay in our own world of ideas and emotions. We are here to serve, not to impose.

Pray about the 'real world' and not just a narrowly 'church world' Be specific in what you pray about, with examples. Pray about what's in the news, naming specific people and places and issues in society. Avoid too many generalizations ('We pray for China'). Make the connections that enable people to see that prayer isn't just a Sunday ritual but a daily opportunity to be in lively contact with a living Lord.

Choose words wisely Be more Radio 2 than Radio 4, and make sure your prayers come over naturally rather than as an essay. Use vivid, memorable words and phrases that catch the imagination and may trespass outside the normal language of the intercessions. Be prepared to paint word-pictures and use images. You can use rich language without being too flowery – the occasional poetic flourish will delight the heart!

Have a clear structure A structure helps most people feel secure; prayers without structure can sometimes seem like an amorphous blancmange of words. A repeated response can help give that structure and security. In the intercessions in this book the intention is that a response is usually possible but not essential. If a response is used it should be repeated at the start so people have got used to it before the prayers really start. Because we don't want people to have to concentrate hard on not forgetting the response, short ones are preferable, and the two most common ones are still very useful: 'Lord, in your mercy, **hear our prayer**' and 'Lord hear us. **Lord, graciously hear us.**' Sometimes it helps for intercessions to have a trajectory, e.g. to start small and local, and then spread out step by step. This gives a sense of direction to the prayers which many find helpful.

Address biddings to the congregation and prayers to God
Confusing these two is one of the most common problems in intercession. It probably doesn't confuse God, but at some level it can confuse the congregation, and it can make the prayer itself feel less sincere. A bidding might start, 'The news of the plane crash yesterday makes our heart break . . .' A prayer, on the other hand, would start, 'Lord, we pray for the victims of yesterday's plane crash . . .' Biddings can be helpful, in part because while God doesn't need to be reminded of the crash, we might. But it's still the *prayer* which actually addresses God and the *bidding* that addresses us.

Pray, don't read notes This is quite tricky, but something is lost when we're obviously reading out the notes we wrote the day before – the authenticity of coming to God with our heartfelt intercessions is diminished. It's the same when a preacher reads out his or her sermon, occasionally looking up from the notes, instead of speaking to the congregation with occasional reference to the notes. One of the things that gives it away if we're reading more than praying is if we say 'it is' instead of 'it's'; we usually *write* the first and *say* the second. With intercessions the key is the direction of the heart. If we are clearly addressing God, bringing God our real needs, it won't matter if the words of the prayers are all written out. But if we're really just addressing the piece of paper in front of us, it will show.

Take a few risks   What initially woke me from my boredom with intercessions was when someone painted a word-picture of some situations in Africa. I was immediately engaged and prayed with sincerity. Why not push the boundaries a little – while of course respecting the needs of the congregation? Could you have a sung response, with choir or music group leading? Could you use a verse from a hymn or song at the beginning and end of the intercessions? Could you use images on the projector and ask people to look at them while they pray? Could you invite the congregation to imagine in their minds a particular person of their choosing and hold that picture before them as they pray? Could you get them to pick up the news-sheet and pray for the list of events through the week, and pray for the mission partner whose photo you've managed to get on to the news-sheet? It's also good to take the risk of using different *styles* of intercession to avoid getting into a rut.

Offer silence   Could you use silence more effectively, giving people real space to say their own prayers? Many of the intercessions in this book give the opportunity for the congregation to pray in their own way in silence. If we're leading intercessions we need to signal clearly that this is what's happening – we're leaving space for personal prayer – and then we need to keep our side of the bargain, and refuse to panic and close the silence down too soon. For many people in the congregation, used to an incessant stream of words in public worship, this silence will be a huge gift. People will weep on your neck with gratitude and bring you flowers. But if you're going to introduce longer periods still, you'll need to work up to it and give more guidance on the use of this unexpected space. In a world of constant noise and distraction, never underestimate how much silence is appreciated.

Look for training and feedback   It's very helpful if the church gathers its intercessors together every now and then to refresh the way they lead intercessions. We can all benefit from training and sharing what works well and what doesn't. It can also be useful to ask trusted friends for feedback on our leading of prayers. They can both affirm and gently point out ways to make our intercessions more helpful. It's a risk, but worth it.

2 WHAT ARE WE DOING WHEN WE INTERCEDE?

This isn't a trivial question. If we aren't sure why we're doing it then we'll lack conviction in our prayers. Similarly, if we have beliefs about what's happening as we pray that seem unbelievable to the congregation then, again, our leading of prayers will lack credibility. So let's look very briefly at two huge questions: what intercession is not, and what intercession is.

WHAT INTERCESSION IS NOT

It's not magic We're not rubbing the genie's lamp and getting what we want, or putting our bank card in the ATM of the Universal Bank of Almighty God. There is, in other words, no guarantee that what we pray for is going to yield a precise response. But on the other hand we can certainly be sure that no prayer is ever *not* answered; we just need to be more alert to a variety of possible responses.

It's not persuading God to do what 'he' (excuse the simplification) would not otherwise have done Our prayer isn't changing God's mind or overcoming his reluctance; it's taking hold of God's willingness and putting our love at God's disposal. We're not telling God anything he doesn't already know and where he isn't already determined to work for the very best outcome. So it isn't necessary in intercession to stack up as much fire-power as possible to breach God's defences. God is already, and always, on our side.

It's not trying to get God to break the 'laws of nature' The Newtonian world-view was very deterministic. The universe was seen as a closed system, a machine where the future could be predicted if you had enough information. The universe of quantum and chaos theory is very different, much more open and unpredictable. In such a universe the 'laws of nature' are regularities, not iron walls of certainty, and God can more easily be understood as actively involved in the life of the world. God is, after all, the Ground of all existence, the Inwardness of all things. Just don't push me to explain it!

It's not just to get us motivated The view is sometimes expressed that the main purpose of prayer is not to change God but to change ourselves. Agreed – it's not trying to change God, but it's more than just giving ourselves a motivational speech. God isn't the deistic God who wound up the mechanism of the universe and now lets it run by itself. God both sustains and involves himself in the warp and weft of creation, an active agent, not a passive principle.

SO WHAT IS INTERCESSION?

Intercession is us co-operating with God in the healing of creation That's the rather grandiose 'big picture'. God's purpose is to 'gather up all things in Christ' (Ephesians 1.10) and God looks for our co-operation, in which prayer has a major part to play. The healing of creation into the perfect integration of heaven and earth is made up of a zillion details, so what we pray for is just a small part of a great enterprise – a world that is good, just, free and at peace. Intercession, then, is working with God in all things to bring about the best outcomes. Prayer is part of a constant conversation between heaven and earth and gives us a place in God's great work of building the kingdom.

Intercession is one of our best ways of loving someone The best and most loving thing we can do for anyone is to put them into the hands of God. God cares for that person's well-being far more than we ever can, but our love is used by God in his good purposes for that person. We never know what love can achieve. It's been said that love would make a significant health difference to a large proportion of the people who occupy our hospital beds. It's an interesting assertion but, whether true or not, who knows what inexhaustible love, God's love, can do in a given situation? Jesus, in his ministry, seems to have experimented with divine love to see what it could achieve, and we do the same in our praying.

We should be prepared for wonderful things to happen when we pray, but to be disappointed too   We don't know what the limits of Almighty Love are. There must be limits in a finite, created world – you can't have dry rain or square circles. God limited himself in the act of creation, as love always has to. But as we don't know where the limits of Almighty Love are, we can pray hopefully about anything and everything, and then leave it to God, who's always working for the best outcomes possible in a finite world. A quantum universe can't be infinitely open, but it's more open than many people think.

God's love is constant   God is always 'on our side' and working for our well-being. Many people have somehow got the idea that God's love is unreliable, inconsistent, or that he's always on the watch to see if we step out of line. Nothing could be further from the truth. God is always rooting for us, cheering us on. 'If God is for us, who is against us? He who did not withhold his own Son, but gave him up for all of us, will he not . . . also give us everything else?' (Romans 8.31–32). God is fundamentally and irrevocably 'with us' every step of the way.

Answers to prayer come in many forms   We often have a simple binary approach – God answered our prayer or he didn't. But relationships are much more subtle than that, and prayer is a relationship, not a mechanism. Answers could come as yes, no, not a good idea, if, let's keep working on this, wouldn't this be better?, hang on a bit, nice try, probably, could you do this?, high-five – all sorts. Like any relationship our responses to each other are much more nuanced than a flat yes or no. But all prayer is answered in some way, just as every child's request receives an answer from a parent – even if not quite the one the child wanted. 'Can a woman forget her nursing-child or show no compassion for the child of her womb?' (Isaiah 49.15). But even if she could, God can't.

Our intercessions aren't faultless!   We don't have the complete picture so we just do our best. But, wonderfully, God has seen that problem coming and, says St Paul, has given the Holy Spirit to pray in us. 'The Spirit helps us in our weakness; for we do not know how to pray as we ought, but that very Spirit intercedes with sighs too deep for words' (Romans 8.26). That takes the pressure off a bit . . .

We don't have to understand how prayer 'works'; we just have to do as Jesus did   And Jesus prayed constantly to his Father. He disappeared whenever he could to be with his Father in prayer, taking to him the needs he had at that time – for resilience facing the temptations of his future ministry, for energy in the midst of a punishing schedule, for wisdom in choosing the twelve disciples, for strength to face the final hurdle. To his disciples, and so to us, he said, 'When you pray, say: "Father, hallowed be your name. Your kingdom come. Give us each day our daily bread . . ."' (Luke 11.2–3).

In those two last phrases is a complete mandate for a ministry of intercession.

3 THROUGH THE YEAR

(1) JANUARY

*Each section could end with: 'Lord, in your mercy, **hear our prayer**' or 'Lord, hear us. **Lord, graciously hear us.**'*

Lord of the year,

In January the festive lights have gone out and darkness lies over the face of the land. We give thanks for every blessing of the past Christmas season, even as we peer uncertainly into the year ahead. Give us the assurance that you will be with us in the future, as deeply as you have been in the past, and that nothing can separate us from your love.

In January we make our New Year resolutions but too often and too soon familiarity drags us back to old habits. Help us to discern what changes really matter, and give us a double portion of your Spirit to make those changes and to keep to them. We pray for those who are bound to addictions they long to break – addictions to alcohol, drugs, gambling, pornography or whatever it is that holds them captive. Give them strength to begin the long journey back to themselves.

In January, while we shiver, the southern hemisphere is in high summer. We pray for the relatives, friends and other people we know in countries in the southern half of the world map, naming them in our hearts now . . . We pray too for those who are desperate to escape danger or poverty in the Global South, and so risk even more danger in making their way north. May they meet understanding and compassion in Europe, even as Europe seeks long-term solutions to its over-popularity.

In January our church looks at the year ahead and how we plan to bear witness to Christ, and how we'll serve our community in the name of Christ. So we pray now for events and programmes coming up in our church life . . .

In January we set our compass afresh on you, our ever-present, ever-loving God. Keep us firm in the hope you have set before us. May we not waver or procrastinate in our discipleship, but enter our new year sharing your joy and singing your song.

God of January, Lord of the year, lead us through this month with faith, hope and love.

(2) FEBRUARY

*Each section could end with: 'Lord, in your mercy, **hear our** **prayer'** or 'Lord, hear us. **Lord, graciously hear us.'***

Gracious God,

We often feel by February that winter has gone on long enough. Cold and darkness have prevailed for months and yet winter sometimes has its sharpest moments during these weeks. But, underground, life is beginning to stir as nature hatches new plans. We pray that, as nature comes to life, you will awaken our sleeping faith as well; so warm our hearts and kindle our hope for joys to come.

In February we celebrate [have celebrated] the feast of St Valentine, and declarations of love are [were] made and enjoyed in myriad ways. We give thanks for the irrepressible gift of human love, giving delight, companionship and comfort – while praying also for those who feel left outside that experience, neglected and unloved by those who matter. Make us agents of your love to everyone we meet this week.

In February our horizons are often closed down as we plod on. February can make life seem predictable and unexciting. And yet we are citizens of a thrilling and fascinating world. Keep our eyes open and our vision high, both for this world and the next. In this world, bless our leaders and our well-worn instruments of government. We ask particularly for wisdom for those in international institutions who have to deliberate over places of intractable need, such as . . . And we ask you to stay the hand of the people of violence in . . .

In February we often experience the ordinariness of life without the highlights of festivals and holidays and summer sun. February drags by. We pray for those for whom every day feels ordinary, those without good health or sufficient money, or without family and friends to love them. In our hearts we name any we know

11

who are struggling . . . This week, help us to notice those who are unnoticed, and to offer time, attention and kindness.

God of February, Lord of the year, lead us through this month with faith, hope and love.

(3) MARCH

Each section could end with: 'Lord, in your mercy, **hear our prayer**' *or* 'Lord, hear us. **Lord, graciously hear us.**'

Gracious God,

In March nature begins to wake up and shake off its winter sleep. Thank you for the purity of the snowdrops, the striking colours of the crocuses, the wavy yellow heads of the early daffodils – such encouragement to eyes bored with brown. Give us hearts full of anticipation as spring arrives, fresh and on time, and again you demonstrate your faithfulness and patience through the natural world. Make us faithful too, both in our relationships and in the way we live our faith.

In March we count the weeks of Lent and wonder if we can keep up with giving up, or keep on what we've taken on. We're supposed to learn self-discipline and the value of commitment, yet too often we learn how fickle we are, and how unprepared even for the sacrifices of love. Take our lives, we pray, and shape them according to your original design. Make them fruitful and joyful as we bend to your gentle persuasion. In silence we offer ourselves again to your guiding hand . . .

In March the hatreds and cruelties of men and women are no less marked than in any other month. Violence continues to destroy lives and dreams in . . . and . . . We're ashamed of our common humanity but we know you will not turn away and reject us. Bring the combatants together, we pray; may their negotiations be as realistic as Lent and as hopeful as spring.

In March we plunge ever closer to the starkness of Holy Week. We pray that many will take that journey with us this year, that many will be touched by the Love that stopped at nothing and made even death lay down its arms. We bring with us on that journey those who suffer and look for healing of body and soul, especially . . . May they know that there's nothing

13

to be afraid of because perfect love casts out fear, and you *are* Perfect Love.

God of March, Lord of the year, lead us through this month with faith, hope and love.

(4) APRIL

*Each section could end with: 'Lord, in your mercy, **hear our prayer**' or 'Lord, hear us. **Lord, graciously hear us.**'*

Gracious God,

In April our gardens are beginning to pick up speed, and new life is emerging daily. We pray for gardeners, both amateur and professional, as they cherish and nurture the gifts you give. We rarely pray for council gardeners who bring beauty to our streets and parks, but we do so now, with thanks for their patient work . . . Give all gardeners pleasure in sun and soil, planting and weeding, and give us all an abiding sense of reverence for nature's gifts.

In April the miracle of Easter has burst upon us, but sadly it vanishes all too soon as we plan spring breaks and begin to feel the lazy warmth of the sun. We pray that you will keep the risen Christ alive in our hearts as we enjoy the lasting truth of Easter. May we see Christ in one another and know his abundant life in all we do.

In April we watch our children and grandchildren getting out of the house and stretching their limbs in sport and play. We pray for the children closest to us, in our families, among our neighbours, in our church. We remember them before you now, silently by name, those closest to us . . . Give these children such stimulus and joy that they never lose their enthusiasm for life. And give their parents and teachers the love and inspiration they also need, day by day.

In April people struggle with illness, bereavement and hard decisions, just like any other month. We call to mind and offer to you now these people whom we carry in our hearts . . . *(church list or personal friends).*

We began April with a Fool's Day. May we be prepared to be fools for Christ, open in our witness, not knowing all the answers, but glad to belong to him and aware of the privilege.

15

May our lives tell the story of our faith and demonstrate the sincerity of our love.

God of April, Lord of the year, lead us through this month with faith, hope and love.

(5) MAY

*Each section could end with: 'Lord, in your mercy, **hear our prayer**' or 'Lord, hear us. **Lord, graciously hear us.**'*

Gracious God,

May means many things to different people. To some it's the Cup Final and the proper start of the cricket season. To others it's the garden and perhaps the first barbecue. For others it's when the National Trust has opened its doors and days out go further than the local shopping mall. Thank you for the variety of ways in which we can enjoy the abundant life that Jesus promised. In everything, may we know the love of Christ and be thankful.

We pray this month for those who depend on tourism for their livelihood, and for whom a bad summer can spell disaster and a good one prosperity. We pray in particular for those who depend on good weather, those who run outdoor attractions, seaside hotels and cafés, those planning fêtes and festivals, those selling ice-cream and cold beer. Bless them this summer, we pray. Give them peace and patience as the weeks go on – and, if necessary, better luck next year . . .

May is the month when in the Christian year we are often celebrating the Ascension and Pentecost, those great festivals that society has largely forgotten. May we know afresh in our lives the liberation of Christ ascended over all things, and the power of the Spirit to change all things, even in us. We pray, therefore, that our most-used prayer may indeed come true, and your kingdom come and your will be done on earth, as it is in heaven.

For some people May is as much of a struggle as April. We pray for those living with long-term, debilitating illness, for the many who live with depression or who write themselves off or practise self-harm. We probably all know some such people and can pray for them now, in our hearts . . . May they know, somehow and possibly through us, that they are infinitely valuable to you, and that you love them with a deep and lasting tenderness.

Loving God, this month belongs to you. Help us to live it fully and graciously, in the company of family and friends and in the fellowship of the Church on earth and in heaven.

God of May, Lord of the year, lead us through this month with faith, hope and love.

(6) JUNE

*Each section could end with: 'Lord, in your mercy, **hear our prayer**' or 'Lord, hear us. **Lord, graciously hear us**'.*

Gracious God,

June takes us into the golden months we've been waiting for with hopes of high summer, cold drinks and warm evenings. It means Wimbledon and the first Test match, people sitting out in street cafés and children playing joyfully in the park. Thank you for the pleasure we have (or have had!) in sport – playing or watching. Thank you for the delight we have in stretching our bodies and testing our limits. May our children and young people experience that same exhilaration in your thrilling gift of life.

June is the month of fêtes and fundraising events. Thank you for those who give themselves faithfully to the planning and organizing of these events. We pray for those who have responsibility for the finances of our churches and charities and the host of voluntary organizations that depend on annual fundraising. Bless them with the sense of a job well done, and above all, bless them with success. We pray especially for . . .

June is the month when our children finish their exams. Help them in the final run-up to exams to stay on task, focus on their revision and get their reward. Help particularly the children and university students who struggle with anxiety over exams and often don't do themselves justice. Give them quiet hearts and quick minds when it really matters. We pray this week for the students at . . .

Gracious God, you have given us a job description that doesn't change: to go in peace, to love and serve the Lord. When we go out this week to a bewildered world, vulnerable ourselves but joyful, help us to lead God-shaped lives that speak peace and hope into the lives of others. In silence now we bring to you some of the particular things we'll be doing this week . . .

19

God of June, Lord of the year, lead us through this month with faith, hope and love.

(7) JULY

*Each section could end with: 'Lord, in your mercy, hear our prayer' or 'Lord, hear us. **Lord, graciously hear us.**'*

Gracious God,

In July summer is upon us and rumours of sunshine prove to be true. We give thanks for the life-giving blaze of the sun pouring over the world, bringing warmth and growth and well-being. But we pray also for people in countries where the sun is so hot and water is so short that the temperatures are life-threatening. As climate change makes the problem worse, we pray for sustained progress towards carbon reduction across the globe. May this not be the generation that ducks the crisis but the one that begins to solve it.

In July schools are out and our children are released to make the most of the summer with their friends. We recognize the importance of social media to younger generations in particular, and pray that, while claiming the benefits of an online world, they may be kept from an unhealthy addiction to it. Help them to sustain genuine relationships and be resilient in the face of cyber-bullying and the pressures of sexting.

In July television adverts and media stories encourage us to be happy, emphasizing smiling families relaxing around barbecues or jetting off to the sun. But we know that many lives are short on sunshine. Summer brings no let-up in the struggle to make ends meet. We pray for the forgotten, voiceless people who long ago gave up holidays and have to concentrate instead on getting food on to their children's plates. Bless those charities that take food poverty seriously, that run food banks and advocate for people who have fallen foul of benefit sanctions. Help us to make this country and its systems fairer and more compassionate.

In July church activities and programmes slow down, unless there are holiday clubs for children or seniors. May this slowing down be a gift to us all. Help us to re-focus on you at the centre of

21

everything we enjoy, you who came in Christ that we might have life and have it abundantly. Remind us why we come to church – so that we will love both you and our neighbour more fully. Keep us to that noble goal as we enjoy now in our prayers a period of stillness to make more space for you in our lives . . . *(prolonged silence)*.

God of July, Lord of the year, lead us through this month with faith, hope and love.

(8) AUGUST

*Each section could end with: 'Lord, in your mercy, **hear our prayer**' or 'Lord, hear us. **Lord, graciously hear us.**'*

Gracious God,

August is the month when we go on holiday and leave the world to look after itself. We pray for those we know on holiday now, for safe travel, good accommodation and wonderful experiences. Bring them back sun-blessed and refreshed, and ready for action in your service. We pray too for those for whom a holiday isn't possible this year. Bless them in their staying put and give them other opportunities for refreshment and renewal.

August reminds us of the importance of a rhythm to life which includes coming and going, giving and receiving, working and resting. May your gift of Sabbath rest be one we incorporate into our lives throughout the year, recognizing the value of living in harmony with ourselves and with others, with nature and with you. We pray for those whose situation or whose temperament pushes them into over-work and insufficient rest. Silently we pray for those we know who are tempted in this way . . .

We pray for those people who have to keep working through the summer season in order to make sure the rest of us are safe – the emergency services, health staff, workers in the power industry, the military. The network of our interdependence is now so delicate we hardly appreciate what's being done for us all the time by so many. Encourage and sustain them, we pray, and give us opportunities to thank them.

As we loosen our grip on our normal routines and cares, we know that you never let go of your concern for those in special need. Among them, we pray for . . . Bring them healing of mind, body and spirit, and the assurance that nothing can separate them from your love.

Finally we offer ourselves to you this week, and look ahead through the week's commitments and events . . . May we meet you in and through all things, and be thankful.

God of August, Lord of the year, lead us through this month with faith, hope and love.

(9) SEPTEMBER

*Each section could end with: 'Lord, in your mercy, **hear our
prayer**' or 'Lord, hear us. **Lord, graciously hear us.**'*

Gracious God,

It's September and change is in the air. Children are back in
school, students are getting ready for university, teachers and
lecturers are shaking themselves down and getting back into
work mode. We pray for those young people who are anxious
about this transition, the strangeness of new classes, new forms
of work, new companions in new places. Give them confidence in
themselves and in the systems they will be part of. And for those
who recognize you as Lord, be their rock and their guide.

In September nature is beginning to move on, stripping back its
summer foliage, but with a final burst of summer fruitfulness.
Our faith too has to move on, not relying on past experience
and yesterday's answers. Make us ready for the journey, moving
on to wherever you may take us, without doubting your loving
presence. Keep us from a stagnant faith that never changes and
grows. Open us to new things this autumn.

Lord, why do people hate when there's so much to love? There
is hatred and fear in . . . and . . ., and it's been going on too
long. We believe that love is stronger than hate because hate
divides and love unites. Take hold of the unruly passions of
sinful men and women, and patiently teach them, and us, the
ways of love.

Lord, we are each here with a bundle of concerns – mistakes
made, tasks unfinished, decisions to be taken, relationships to
attend to, people on our hearts. We bring these bundles to you
and ask for your kindness and wisdom. Help us to give proper
attention to these things, not to duck them or keep them to
ourselves, but to open them to you for you to touch them with
your lively wisdom and grace. We pray in quiet now for what is
chiefly on our hearts at the start of this week . . .

Lord, we believe; help our unbelief.

God of September, Lord of the year, lead us through this month with faith, hope and love.

(10) OCTOBER

Each section could end with: 'Lord, in your mercy, hear our prayer' or 'Lord, hear us. Lord, graciously hear us.'

Gracious God,

In October we take delight in the rich colours of autumn that startle the senses with their bold extravagance. May we never cease to marvel at nature's palette and be dazzled by every burning bush that speaks of your glory.

In October we enjoy the last fruits of the earth's generosity this year. May we in turn be generous in our care for this good earth and make it our concern that every species of bird, animal, tree and plant survives and flourishes in its own way. We pray for all the organizations and individuals committed to conservation and care of the environment, in particular the Christian organization A Rocha. May we be among those committed to the environment, and demonstrate our determination not to harm the world as we journey through it.

In October, with summer gone, we turn our minds to the hard realities that never went away – those of politics and finance, global security and international peace. We pray for all those called to high and heavy responsibility in national life, especially . . .

In October holidays seem long ago and Christmas far away. We pray for the life of the church through these weeks, that we may each contribute to the church's life in the best way we can, and that our life together may be attractive and Christ-centred, enabling us to live fully in *your* world in *your* way with *your* help. Especially we pray for . . . *(aspects of church life)*.

For some in October hearts are heavy and heads hang down. Encourage those who are facing hard times, difficult decisions, problematic relationships or uncertain health. Touch their lives with hope and assure them that nothing can separate them from your love. Especially we pray for . . . *(church list or personal concerns)*.

God of October, Lord of the year, lead us through this month with faith, hope and love.

(11) NOVEMBER

*Each section could end with: 'Lord, in your mercy, **hear our prayer**' or 'Lord, hear us. **Lord, graciously hear us.**'*

Gracious God,

In November the natural world is closing down for winter. The days are getting shorter and a chill slides under the door. Help us not to close down our hopes and dreams, our warmth and welcome. Keep us hospitable to others and open to you.

In November Guy Fawkes makes a noisy, colourful appearance that reminds us of unhappier times in relations between the Churches. Bless, we pray, our Roman Catholic brothers and sisters and all our work together for the kingdom of God.

In November we remember in serious silence the anguish and carnage of war, and reflect again on our capacity for hatred and violence. Hold back, we pray, the people of war, encourage and strengthen the people of peace, and give hope especially to . . . *(places in the news)*.

In November we turn our thoughts towards Christmas and who will go to whom this year and what we'll do about cards and presents. In our churches, help us to hold back on Christmas and to make proper space first for Advent, and in society as a whole, help us to make proper space for kindness, generosity and care for the outsider as the race for Christmas gathers speed. In our church life we pray for . . .

In November we pray for those for whom this month brings memories of loss, and for those who suffer from depression and the absence of light. Give them your own light, we pray, and especially to those in prisons, in psychiatric hospitals and in their own dark places. In your light may they see light – and the stirrings of hope.

We offer ourselves to you this week and pray that we may find you in all things and all people, and respond to you with grace and gratitude.

God of November, Lord of the year, lead us through this month with faith, hope and love.

(12) DECEMBER

*Each section could end with: 'Lord, in your mercy, **hear our
prayer**' or 'Lord, hear us. **Lord, graciously hear us.**'*

Gracious God,

In December the trees are bare at last, the ground cold and hard.
Random weather events disturb our best-laid plans, and we relish
the warm welcome of our homes. Be present, we pray, in these
darker days as we hunker down and wait for the light that shines
from Bethlehem's cave.

In December the engines of industry are working flat out to
earn the long Christmas break. Bless those who make cars and
widgets, those who handle money and insurance, those who
design and innovate and re-imagine our future – all contributing
to the well-being of the nation. But remind us also that we do not
live by GDP alone but by the light that shines from Bethlehem's
cave.

In church throughout December we light our Advent candles and
plan our alternative to society's secular festival. Give us patience,
imagination and the odd stroke of genius in that planning, so that
we might hold out afresh the Word of Life, full of grace and truth
from Bethlehem's cave.

In December we count our blessings and mourn our losses. We
love the Christmas season, and dread it. It comes as forecast – a
huge tide of consumer spending and exhausting pleasure that
recedes as quickly as does any tide. Yet we pray that the tide
may leave behind in many lives signs of renewed joy and restored
hope, flowing irrepressibly from Bethlehem's cave.

We pray for peace around that cave in Palestine, peace in our
world and peace in our restless hearts. Especially we pray for
these places, for . . . *(places in the news)*.

God of December, Lord of the year, lead us through this month
with faith, hope and love.

31

4 SEASONS AND FESTIVALS

(13) ADVENT 1

*A possible verse and response would be 'Lord of our Advent journey, **hear our prayer**'.*

O come, O come, Emmanuel. Come and renew our faith this Advent. Awaken our hearts to the message of the prophet Isaiah that we should make a straight path for you to re-enter our crooked world and our confused lives. Fill us with such confidence in your presence, always and everywhere, that we may live fully and gladly in your world, always facing towards grace.

Lord of our Advent journey, **hear our prayer**.

O come, O come, Emmanuel. Come to a frightened world with hope and courage. Let us hear again your favourite words – 'Do not be afraid'. We recognize the ferocity of humanity's hatreds, and we pray for your mercy on the people of . . . and the refugees in . . . Equip the peacemakers with wise judgement and a calm spirit, and keep them ever hopeful of patient progress.

Lord of our Advent journey, **hear our prayer**.

O come, O come, Emmanuel. Come to those who feel empty of love. Too many people are lonely in our crowded country; too many are unvisited, unknown. Enable us to love our neighbour with the kindness that goes the extra mile, that seeks out the lonely and notices the closed curtains. And enable our church to be a place of warmth, welcome and hospitality for all. We pray in silence now for people we may have neglected . . .

Lord of our Advent journey, **hear our prayer**.

O come, O come, Emmanuel. Come to a forgetful world and remind them of your endless love. We are born seekers, but many people pretend they 'have it all' and have no need of transcendence. Yet you leave your gracious footprints all over creation. May the dawning light of Advent steal across the minds and hearts of many in our community as Christmas comes. And help us, in our turn, to fill Christmas with Christ and help others to feel invited to your party.

Lord of our Advent journey, **hear our prayer.**

Come, Lord Jesus, as we prepare our own hearts for your Advent. This week, give us time for reflection, space for prayer and a hunger for more of you in our lives.

So come, O come, Emmanuel.

(14) ADVENT 2

A familiar response could be used.

Most of us are used to Advent calendars. Imagine this morning that we're opening some of the windows in our Advent calendar and seeing not chocolates or animals, but the things we and the world really need.

In our Advent calendar we open a window on to what we need most: we open a window on to *love*. Help us, good Lord, to notice those who have a love-shaped hole in their lives. There are many such people around us, but often they wear a mask, and often we are too preoccupied to see the loneliness, the unlovedness. May your love be our love, and our love a gift that changes someone's life this week.

In our Advent calendar we open a window on to *joy*, the joy that in a few weeks will overtake shepherds outside Bethlehem, inspire wise men from the east, and release Simeon and Anna from their faithful vigil. Help us, good Lord, to offer joy to the worlds we inhabit – our homes and places of work, our clubs, groups and voluntary organizations, our families and friends. We see many on the streets or in the supermarkets who look anxious, harassed and far from the abundant life you offer. May we be agents of joy to others – and to ourselves – by the way we smile, greet people, listen and share the joy of the coming Christ child. Show us, good Lord, who we might share that joy with this week.

In our Advent calendar we open a window on to *peace*, praying for a world that often seems to have forgotten how to live in peace and harmony. Our hearts go out to . . . *(places in the news)*, where violence and hatred snarl in the face of peace. Help us to keep sorrow company but always look hopefully towards peace. And in our own lives help us to demonstrate an uncalculating generosity to all people, for in every person you come as Christ into our lives. Show us, good Lord, if there is anyone with whom we need to make peace this week.

In our Advent calendar we open a window on to *a sleeping child in a manger.* There we see a fullness and kindness that the world has never known before. Here is a child destined to grow into the wonder of his life, even as he faces the terrible nightmare of the cross. As we journey through Advent, make us determined to conform our lives to the life of this soon-to-be-born Saviour, in whom everything is blessed. We look now through the week ahead, its appointments, its opportunities and its threats, and we ask for grace to live well as we follow the path of Jesus . . . *(space for reflection).*

Gracious God, we put down our Advent calendar with its gifts of love, joy, peace and a sleeping child – until tomorrow, when we shall see once more how much you promise us, in Jesus Christ our Lord.

(15) ALL SAINTS

*At All Saints-tide we celebrate the saints of old but also the saints of today in other parts of the world and those sitting around us in church. These intercessions bring the presence of saints up to date and so could be used at other times of the year as well. A familiar response could be used, or 'For all the saints, **we give our thanks and praise'**.*

God of infinite grace, thank you for scattering saints all over the Church: saints in heaven, saints on earth, saints in our lives, saints in this church, and saints who never try to be anything other than themselves but to us are dipped in grace. Thank you for a world of saints – some of whom we have revered in history, and some of whom we have known ourselves and name in our hearts now . . .

For all the saints, **we give our thanks and praise.**

God of deep memory, we look back in gratitude to the saints of old who trod these paths and hallowed them, setting their lives over the template of Christ. Heaven is bursting with these saints and we often wonder whether men and women are made like that any more. But St Paul says that all Christians are called to be saints, set apart for faithful living. We pray, then, for ourselves and those sitting around us today. Humbly we pray that you will mould us into the likeness of Christ, the true goal of our lives.

For all the saints, **we give our thanks and praise.**

God of huge abundance, thank you for saints whose laughter lights up a meeting, for saints whose joy makes us smile just to think of them, for saints whose sacrifice makes us humble, for saints whose lives make us search our consciences, for saints whose prayer helps sustain the world. We know that saints have been in the making all their lives – as have those who have grumbled their way to the present. So make us a church that practises wisdom and honours prayer, so that all who worship here may know themselves to belong to a school of sinners who

36

are training to be saints. Thank you for a world of saints; please make more of them.

For all the saints, **we give our thanks and praise.**

God of the nations, we pray for saints across the world living on the edge of safety but practising their faith with fierce love and deep commitment. We think particularly of Christians in . . . We are humbled by their sincerity and dedication, and are honoured to pray for them, especially for Christians with whom we have links across the world . . . *(name any links the church has)*. Make them strong in faith and love, and protect them on every side.

For saints across the ages, and for saints of today, we give our thanks and praise.

(16) CHRISTMAS 1

The response to the words 'Hark, the herald angels sing' is 'Glory to the new-born King'.

Eternal God, you have given us so many gifts and now the greatest gift of all. Your love for us and all creation is expressed in the beauty and vulnerability of a new-born child. Our joy is sung by the angels. Our presence in the story is seen in ordinary shepherds. Our homage is made by those men from the east. In amazement we can only say 'thank you' – and continue telling the story.

Hark, the herald angels sing: **Glory to the new-born King**.

Christmas isn't just for the children, but it *is* for children. Thank you for their innocent excitement which reminds us of what we've often lost. Bless them not just with presents but with Jesus. May their lives be touched by his life, their story connect with his. We pray, naming them now in our hearts, for children who are special in our lives, for their joy, their future, their faith . . .

Hark, the herald angels sing: **Glory to the new-born King**.

Christmas isn't just for adults, but it *is* for adults. We may have grown jaded from many Christmases. We may have become disappointed by the loss of magic and fallen back into more worldly celebrations. Speak to us afresh through the simplicity of the story and the extraordinary truth it contains, and in that freshness call us back to be 'detectives of divinity', seeking your presence anywhere and everywhere, even in ourselves. May Christmas make us different this year . . .

Hark, the herald angels sing: **Glory to the new-born King**.

As well as glory there's also sadness at Christmas: sadness for those left behind by neglect, loneliness, bereavement, messy relationships and more. There are no easy, 'over-the-counter' solutions to the smudge and stain of our struggles, but we pray for the transforming presence everywhere of the Christ child, this down-to-earth God, with his gift of life and hope. We name in our hearts any who will be finding this time hard . . . For these people too we say,

Hark, the herald angels sing: **Glory to the new-born King.**

At Christmas divine lightning strikes the earth and nothing is the same again. This is the heart-stopping moment when 'Before Christ' changed to 'Anno Domini', BC to AD, and we are invited to the birthday party of a new world. Lord, as far as we are able, we accept the invitation. Thank you, we'll be there.

Hark, the herald angels sing: **Glory to the new-born King.**

(17) CHRISTMAS 2

*It could be particularly effective if a solo voice sang the verse of
the carol at the beginning and end of the intercessions. In between
the sections of the prayers the response is: 'What can I give him?*
Give my heart.*'*

> What can I give him, poor as I am?
> If I were a shepherd I would bring a lamb;
> if I were a wise man, I would do my part.
> Yet what I can I give him: give my heart.

This lovely season we give our heart to children. In the child in the
manger we see all children, beautiful and blessed, every child full
of possibilities. And yet we mess them up. Forgive us, good Lord,
and help us to treasure our children above all else, to be tender
and kind, protective and encouraging. We pray for children in
poorer countries denied the benefits of education, healthcare and
security. These are your children; may they be our children too.

What can I give him? **Give my heart.**

This lovely season we give our hearts to family and friends. The
child in the manger had devoted parents who loved him to bits.
Later he had brothers and sisters and friends of the family. We
give thanks for our families, whether with us now or fondly
remembered. And in the silence, let us pray for them, for their
needs now or for their life in glory . . .

What can I give him? **Give my heart.**

This lovely season we give our hearts to generosity. The child in
the manger was brought presents from distant lands; perhaps a
shepherd brought a lamb. We buy presents and prepare the best
meals we can. We greet distant friends and colleagues in a spirit
of welcome and trust. We practise goodwill to all and forgiveness
for past hurts. We pray, good Lord, for this spirit of generosity
to flow into next year, subverting family arguments, industrial
disputes and political animosity. May we give our hearts to
generosity.

What can I give him? **Give my heart.**

This lovely season we give our hearts to justice and joy. The child in the manger grew up and took the side of the excluded and forgotten, inviting them into the joy of his Father's banquet. Make us like Jesus, we pray, always leaning towards those on the margins, on the streets, on the edge. We pray for those without homes today, for Crisis and its Christmas dinners, for those watching television alone, for those remembering loved ones lost. We pray now for any we know for whom this is a hard time . . .

> What can I give him, poor as I am?
> If I were a shepherd I would bring a lamb;
> if I were a wise man I would do my part.
> Yet what I can I give him: **give my heart.**

41

(18) EPIPHANY

*The following response, or any other, could be used: 'Eternal God, Lord of the nations, **hear our prayer**.'*

Eternal God, you invited wise men to represent the nations at the birth of your Son. So call the nations now to hear that invitation afresh and to come not just to bring gifts but to receive the gift of peace from the Prince of Peace. We pray for groups throughout the world, trapped in adolescent hatreds and working them out in repression and violence. In particular we pray for . . . *(current troublespots)*.

Eternal God, Lord of the nations, **hear our prayer**.

The wise men brought gold, recognizing the special nature of this child. May the wealth of the world be distributed more fairly and not mired in corruption and greed. May our bankers and financiers be held firm by moral principle and by respect for the people they serve. And may we all use our own wealth, great or small, with generosity and wisdom. In silence let us pray for our own bank, its leaders and its policies . . .

Eternal God, Lord of the nations, **hear our prayer**.

The wise men brought frankincense because they recognized the divine character of this child. In a world where all such special claims are contested, bring many to look again at the person of Christ and there to glimpse your self-portrait, given to us to be example, Saviour and Lord of our lives. In silence let us pray for any of our family and friends who we long to see come to know the reality of Christ . . .

Eternal God, Lord of the nations, **hear our prayer**.

The wise men brought myrrh, unconsciously recognizing the destiny of this child in untimely death. May the reality of the destiny that faces us all encourage us to live well in this world, filling each day with value, and seeking the well-being of our neighbour. There are many around the world who will have to let

42

go of this life today. Bless them in this letting go, and those who care for them, and those who will miss them dreadfully.

Eternal God, Lord of the nations, **hear our prayer.**

Lord of the nations, you called wise men to welcome your Son in the early days of his life and to bring him gifts. We know that the only gift Jesus really wants from us is our intention to follow him. Help us to bring that gift now, however robust or tentative we may feel in our faith, for you are a God of infinite welcome and you take us as we are.

> Take my will, and make it thine:
> it shall be no longer mine;
> take my heart: it is thine own,
> it shall be thy royal throne.

(19) LENT 1

The response between each section could be: 'Lenten Lord . . .
hear our prayer.'

In Lent we recognize how hard it is to fly straight in a crooked
world. We pray for those who are caught up in compromise,
whether in business, in politics or in relationships. Give them, we
pray, a plumb-line by which to recognize the truth, and help them
to pursue honesty, loyalty and faithfulness. We pray for such
people and situations of our own knowledge or experience, or
people in the news, or even for ourselves . . .

Lenten Lord, **hear our prayer.**

In Lent we ask again what you require of us, and we get the same
answer – 'to do justice, to love kindness and to walk humbly with
our God'. May that call ring true in the life of our church. Keep
us turned outwards in service of others and inwards in love of
you. In our own church life we pray particularly for . . .

Lenten Lord, **hear our prayer.**

It's been said that Lent is Easter in disguise, but remind us,
good Lord, that Easter doesn't come cheaply, that Lent can't be
trivialized. Ask us the hard questions of Lent – how are we living
before you? How does it go with our soul? If we have to give
things up, enable us. If we have to take things on, show us. If we
have to relish life more fully, give us opportunity.

Lenten Lord, **hear our prayer.**

Lent reminds us of our own poverty, if we measure wealth in
terms of spiritual well-being, emotional maturity and moral
confidence. But we pray also for those who know the sharp
poverties of money, livelihood, opportunity and health. We pray
especially for those who are ill and uncertain about the future,
for those facing medical treatment this week, and for those whose
lives have been reduced to a bed and a chair. We bring particular
people to you now . . .

Lenten Lord, **hear our prayer.**

Help us, Lord, to be attentive this Lent, to listen to our hearts, to the preoccupations of others, and to your quiet voice speaking through everything. We are so easily distracted, so keep us on the case, being attentive, listening to the truth, loving. Here, Lord, is a token of our attentiveness – a minute of silent prayer, bringing our lives before you, asking for grace . . . *(silence for a full minute)*.

Lenten Lord, **hear our prayer.**

(20) LENT 2

The Bible verse at the beginning of each section could be spoken by a different voice. A familiar verse and response could be used.

'Rend your hearts and not your clothing. Return to the LORD, your God, for he is gracious and merciful.'

Lord, we return to you again in Lent and ask you to spring-clean our lives. Sweep through the closed rooms of our hearts where the dust of resentment and the cobwebs of self-pity have gathered. Clear out the excess that keeps us from simplicity, and the rubbish that accumulates in the attic of our mind. Give us a pure focus on you, on your grace, mercy and peace.

'Is not this the fast that I choose: to loose the bonds of injustice, to undo the thongs of the yoke, to let the oppressed go free?'

Lord, release us from our obsession with ourselves and our own desires, and raise our sights to a world of injustice that needs a constant critique from people of faith and goodwill. Help us to look the world in the eye, to expose corruption and hold our leaders to account, so that the poor are not sacrificed on the altar of our greed. Especially we pray for . . . *(current issues, e.g. government aid programme, international trade agreements, banks, etc.).*

'One does not live by bread alone but by every word that comes from the mouth of God.'

Teach us, good Lord, to listen to your voice, redolent with truth among the siren voices of our time. We pray for our politicians, advertisers, journalists and opinion-formers, that they may resist the temptations of a post-fact, post-truth world, and seek only the wisdom that withstands compromise and cowardice, for your word stands tall in a field of half-truths. In particular, now, we pray for . . . *(people in the news).*

'If any want to become my followers, let them deny themselves and take up their cross and follow me.'

46

The world sees all sorts of problems with self-denial, voluntary sacrifice and following anything other than our own instincts. Enable us so to live the truth of your invitation that we can commend with integrity the faith that empowers us and the Lord who captivates us. May our lives tell the story we long to share.

'Create in me a clean heart, O God, and put a new and right spirit within me.'

Good Lord, purify our priorities this Lent as we pursue that clean heart and right spirit. As we live under the dazzling gaze of your love, help us to return that gaze with joy and so be drawn into the generous flow of your grace forever pouring out into the world. This Lent may our hearts be re-fixed on you, O God, and on following the way of your Son, Jesus Christ our Lord.

> We pray for our King, Charles + for his recovery

We pray for our town, our churches, and all those who live here at Brylease Court We ask that you will protect them + surround them with your love

(21) PALM SUNDAY

Possible response: 'Hosanna to the Son of David! **Blessed is he who comes in the name of the Lord.***'*

Lord Jesus, on that momentous day a donkey carried you into Jerusalem. Let it be our privilege to carry you into today's Jerusalems, our world of trouble and terror. Let us bear your weight and be agents of your peace as you bring your kind judgement to a fallen world. We pray in particular for . . . *(places in the news).*

Hosanna to the Son of David! **Blessed is he who comes in the name of the Lord.**

Lord Jesus, the crowd cut branches from the trees to celebrate the arrival of their king. May we daily celebrate your arrival and continued presence in every part of life. May we plant your standard in every place: every office, every home, every school, every relationship. Above all, we celebrate your arrival every day at the doorway of our lives. Come, Lord Jesus, and be our King.

Hosanna to the Son of David! **Blessed is he who comes in the name of the Lord.**

Lord Jesus, the crowd spread their cloaks on the road before you. Help us to spread before you our cloaks of pride and self-sufficiency, the self-absorption that keeps us in a continual stand-off with your love and humility. Help us to take off our masks and silence our endless self-justification, so that we encounter you face to face, full of grace and truth.

Hosanna to the Son of David! **Blessed is he who comes in the name of the Lord.**

Lord Jesus, it was on a donkey that you came, not a warhorse. In all our interactions with people this week may we demonstrate the humility of the man on the donkey and be committed to the well-being of family, friends and neighbours. So we pray now for those we carry in our hearts who are facing particular challenges in their lives . . .

48

Hosanna to the Son of David! **Blessed is he who comes in the name of the Lord.**

But, Lord Jesus, all is not well. We see it in your eyes. This entry is going to lead to disaster and we're going to lose you. Truly there is no 'good' in 'goodbye'. Comfort us with the truth this day: the truth that love is dangerous but beyond price; the truth that our corkscrew hearts cannot be straightened without hurt, but that they *can* be healed, and will be. We bring to you now our own particular deceits and evasions, known only to us and to you . . .

Hosanna to the Son of David! **Blessed is he who comes in the name of the Lord.**

Lord Jesus, you come in the name of the Lord your God. Welcome, Lord; welcome to the divided city of our hearts.

49

(22) GOOD FRIDAY 1

Services on Good Friday often don't have a place for normal intercessions. The focus is really on the Crucified One and how we are implicated in his death. If something like the following is used, there could be a response such as: 'Lord, hear our prayer, and let our cry come unto you.'

What can we say on the day that God died? That we're sorry? That we didn't mean it? Sadly, we did mean it; humanity rebelled against goodness, couldn't stand Love in its pure, uncut form. Lord, forgive our collective madness; restore our belief in Love.

Lord, hear our prayer, **and let our cry come unto you.**

What can we say on the day the light of the world was put out? That we prefer darkness? That we like to stumble and fall? Sadly, too often we slope off into the shadows, hoping others won't see what we do or think or imagine in our hearts. Lord, in the evil of the cross, help us to see the cost of darkness and resolve to resist the dying of the light.

Lord, hear our prayer, **and let our cry come unto you.**

What can we say on the day that tragedy and chaos took over the world? That it's inevitable? That we do our best? Sadly, we don't do our best to hold back the forces of violence and destruction; we let them loose with outrageous regularity. Lord, make us determined always and everywhere to work for the ways of peace, to support and pray for the peacemakers, the United Nations, the aid agencies, and to be people of peace ourselves.

Lord, hear our prayer, **and let our cry come unto you.**

What can we say on the day that God became the victim and perished in the dark? That it was his fault? That he should have tried harder? Sadly, that's what we often say to victims: that they didn't work hard enough, look nice enough or live in the right part of the world. Lord, help us to understand the causes of need and the struggles of the victim. Make us alert to the facts behind the news and open to the compassion of the cross.

Lord, hear our prayer, **and let our cry come unto you.**

What can we say as we survey the glorious wreckage of Golgotha? Nothing, really. All we can do is keep silent and wonder. Wonder at such love, and wonder when we will turn again and be healed.

(23) GOOD FRIDAY 2

Another voice could be used for the first words describing the objects at the cross.

The cross of Jesus is littered with the debris of cruelty and infamy. But each object has a symbolic value in our prayers on Good Friday, the day when prayer seems so inadequate.

There were nails.

Jesus, how those nails must have tortured you. You had to pull yourself up on them in order to breathe, and that only increased the exquisite pain. Forgive us for nailing you down because you were just too much for us, too free, too complete a human being. Forgive us now for trying to nail Love down so that it doesn't run amok and change the world. Forgive us for the way we nail each other down, lest someone else gain an advantage. Forgive us for the nails.

There were thorns.

Jesus, that crown of thorns was meant to hurt and mock. What kind of hopeless king wears a crown of thorns? Forgive us for crowning so many wrong things and failing to crown the King of Glory. We crown power and wealth and celebrity. We don't crown humility and compassion and sacrifice. Forgive us for refusing to recognize you as our true King and your kingdom as our true destiny – heaven come to earth, life for all, for ever. Forgive us for the crown of thorns.

There was vinegar.

Jesus, the vinegar was a nasty taunt. You were so thirsty, and they gave you something undrinkable. Forgive us for giving you the undrinkable residue of our sin and selfishness. There you were, thirsting for us, for our response, and all we could come up with was vinegar. Forgive us for turning away from love, from your divine thirst. Forgive us for the vinegar.

There were dice.

Jesus, the soldiers played dice beneath the cross, so little did they care for the man who loved and forgave them, so little did they understand what was really being played out that day. Forgive us for playing dice in our world when so many important things are at stake. We entertain ourselves to death while others really are dying in sadness and poverty and neglect. Forgive us for our selfish addictions, our superficiality, our tightly bandaged brokenness. Forgive us for the dice.

There was a seamless robe.

Jesus, they even stripped you of your robe. Nakedness was part of the humiliation. A robe that had kept you warm and protected you and was once touched by a woman in a crowd, desperate to be healed of her haemorrhage. A seamless robe, a thing of beauty, just as your Father's purposes of love have always been seamless, from Eden to Bethlehem, from Galilee to Gethsemane to Golgotha – seamless love, seamlessly rejected. Jesus, forgive us for the seamless robe.

Jesus, we watch you die this day, surrounded by the debris of hatred – nails and thorns and vinegar and dice. And yet you gather up the fragments of our sin and take them into the heart of the Father, where they disappear, melting in the furnace of his love.

Thank you, Lord. Thank you.

(24) EASTER 1

*Possible response: 'You are risen. **We are risen. Alleluia!**'*

Risen Lord Jesus, you were an early riser that first Easter morning; you needed no alarm to raise you from your three-day slumber. The engines of creation went into reverse and you rose, scattering to the winds the remnants of death. Raise us, we pray, from the slumber of our too-easy faith and put us to work in the garden of your new creation.

You are risen. **We are risen. Alleluia!**

Risen Lord Jesus, you caught the world by surprise when you broke the steel cords of death. Help us to believe that all things are possible, that nations can make peace, that men and women can love their enemies, that justice can prevail and the meek can inherit the earth. Make us part of the revolution that your resurrection began, especially as we pray for . . . *(places in the news).*

You are risen. **We are risen. Alleluia!**

Risen Lord Jesus, you have given us thousands of mornings, but none like this. Give us eyes to see the outline of the new world that your disciples began to see that day. Help us to see all of life in the light that streams from the empty tomb. Help us to hear the captives' song of freedom and to taste the sweetness of release as eyes are opened and lives are made whole. We pray for any we know who are trapped in difficult situations and long for a way out of the tomb in which they feel imprisoned . . .

You are risen. **We are risen. Alleluia!**

Risen Lord Jesus, you met your special friends at precisely their point of need – Mary Magdalene, Thomas, the two walking to Emmaus, Peter at the lakeside. And to each you brought hope and the promise of life in abundance. Meet us, your Church, in the same way, with hope and abundant life, so that we can bask in the light of your resurrection and reflect that light into a muddled world.

You are risen. **We are risen. Alleluia!**

Risen Lord Jesus, may this Easter story echo afresh around the world and bring millions to wonder, and to weep with joy, at the entrance of the empty tomb.

You are risen. **We are risen. Alleluia!**

(25) EASTER 2

*Another voice could be used for the words that start each section. A familiar verse and response could be used, or: 'Thine be the glory, **risen, conquering Son.**'*

The Easter story is full of powerful symbols that provide starting points for prayer. In our prayers we follow where they lead.

There was a stone that had been rolled away.

Risen Jesus, the stone over your tomb was no match for resurrection. It had to succumb to the power of a new creation breaking out of a grave. Most of us have tombs across which a stone lies heavy and unmoved – tombs in which lie our fears and resentments, our buried sins and unsafe desires, our unhealed memories and unforgiven insults. We remember now our own sealed tombs . . . Roll away the stones from these tombs, we pray. Give us new strength and resolve, and release us into a new day of freedom and joy.

Thine be the glory, **risen, conquering Son.**

There were cloths that had wrapped Jesus' body.

The body had gone. Those strips of cloth were lying empty and flat, no longer enclosing the beloved body that the women had come to anoint. Risen Jesus, we often wrap up our lives in the safety of different cloths that mask our insecurity – cloths of status, qualifications, a healthy bank balance, a full diary. But these cloths are like bandages, covering our wounds. Help us gently to unwind our defences and to stand before you and the world covered in the only thing that matters: the love and compassion of God our Father. May our identity rest only in you.

Thine be the glory, **risen, conquering Son.**

There was a gardener at dawn.

Mary thought you were the gardener, and she was right. You are the gardener of the new world that the resurrection has brought into being. This is the eighth day of creation. Help us as we help others to live in that new reality, confident that now new things are always possible and in the meantime we need not be afraid. May that conviction sink deep into our souls and be a source of endless hope.

Thine be the glory, **risen, conquering Son.**

There were wounds in Jesus' hands and side.

Thomas needed hard evidence and there it was. Resurrection doesn't involve the magical removal of past wounds and the wiping out of our history, but something more – the transformation of that history into something beautiful. Risen Jesus, take our hidden history with all its joy, pain and failure, and make it radiant, evidence of what resurrection can do today. And what we pray for ourselves we pray too for those we love . . .

Thine be the glory, **risen, conquering Son.**

There was a simple meal at Emmaus.

A moment before, he had been there, sharing this simple meal. And now he had disappeared and reality had lurched sideways. This ordinary meal had revealed something extraordinary. Risen Jesus, be with us at our table when we entertain our friends and family. Reveal to us the joy of shared stories and deepening relationships, the result of your presence in the simple fellowship of tables. And may our homes be as open as that home at Emmaus so that we may be able to entertain you in our midst.

Thine be the glory, **risen, conquering Son.**

Risen Jesus, through that stone, those cloths, that garden, those wounds, that meal, you made real your resurrection. Make real your resurrection in us, and may we live that resurrection now and always.

(26) SUNDAYS AFTER EASTER

A possible verse and response would be 'We have been raised with Christ **and seek the things that are above'** *(based on Colossians 3.1).*

Risen Christ, Easter has passed and so quickly we forget the marvellous story and return to mediocrity. We forget the breath-taking message that you are risen and with us, our companion on all our journeys to Emmaus. We forget the new life available to us from that day on. Remind us daily that we are an Easter people, living in the light of the resurrection, enlivened by joy and empowered by love.

We have been raised with Christ **and seek the things that are above.**

Risen Christ, in the winter of this world's wraths and sorrows, come like spring to bring hope to the desperate nations of the world. Our news reports are full of . . . *(e.g. fighting in . . ., terrible famine in . . .).* We often turn away in despair. But you, O Christ, are our first glimpse of a new world where swords will be beaten into ploughshares and spears into pruning-hooks. Keep our leaders hopeful and determined as they work for peace and plenty, often against huge odds. Plant Easter in their hearts.

We have been raised with Christ **and seek the things that are above.**

Risen Christ, we know many people who are living through their own Good Friday, having to face great problems, and feeling abandoned and alone under an iron-grey sky. Open that sky, we pray; let a shaft of Easter light pierce the gloom and illuminate at least part of their landscape. In our hearts we name and pray for some of the people we know who are most troubled, who have most to deal with at present . . . Please also break the ice around our hearts, and make us part of the answer to our own prayers for friends and others in need.

We have been raised with Christ **and seek the things that are above.**

Risen Christ, may our church be an oasis of Easter in our community, a place of life, laughter, play and creativity. May it be a place where people let down their guard and know themselves to be gifted and valued. May it be a place where imaginations fly and hope sings. May it be a place where we do something beautiful for God each week, and then go out as Easter people to serve the community around us – because:

We have been raised with Christ **and seek the things that are above.**

(27) ASCENSION 1

A possible response would be: 'Ascended Lord, in your mercy, hear our prayer.'

Ascension – not feet disappearing into the sky but a life embraced by God, a life returned, fulfilled, complete. Lord, lift our vision above the poverty of our primitive imaginations to celebrate the life, death and new life of Jesus, who now is Christ, for us and for the world.

Ascended Lord, in your mercy, **hear our prayer.**

Ascension – not the loss of Jesus but the gift of an ascended Lord, established in victory over everything that would destroy him. Lift our vision, we pray, to see that victory comes in many forms, and often through suffering. We pray for Christians who are suffering today for their faithfulness, reviled and attacked, sometimes bombed and imprisoned, especially in the Middle and Far East . . . *(current issues and troubled lands where Christians are under pressure).*

Ascended Lord, in your mercy, **hear our prayer.**

Ascension – not an act of dominance but an expression of the power of love. Lord, this is where you are meant to be, at the right hand of the Father; and this is where we are meant to be, followers and witnesses, living the faith and loving our neighbour. All around us our neighbours have needs we're aware of but often we feel unable to help. Prayer is one special way to help, so we pray now for particular neighbours who are having difficulties at present . . .

Ascended Lord, in your mercy, **hear our prayer.**

Ascension – not Jesus leaving home but Jesus returning home to the Father. Thank you for what home means to us – security, acceptance, warmth, comfort. We pray for the many who are homeless even in our advanced society, sleeping out in dangerous doorways or miserable lodgings. Thank you for those

60

organizations and individuals who try to address the complex issues that homeless people often have. Most of us see homeless people or sellers of the *Big Issue* in our city streets, the tip of a very large iceberg. We pray for some of them now, those we have seen recently . . .

Ascended Lord, in your mercy, **hear our prayer.**

Ascension – not as we see it in stained-glass windows, but as we know it in our hearts. The drama of Jesus' life has ended. The drama of his life *in us* has only just begun.

(28) ASCENSION 2

Ascension gets too little recognition, partly because it falls on a Thursday, but more because people don't know what to make of it. This intercession makes the case for Ascension as a 'big ticket' festival and a vehicle for prayer for the whole world. A suitable verse and response would be: 'Lord of all, to you we pray.'

Ascended Lord, at the right hand of the Father, you tower over time, and all things find their fulfilment in you. And yet you ask, in all humility and without pressure, to be Lord of our lives too. Give us the good sense to say yes, to let your presence fill us with gratitude and your graceful wisdom direct our lives.

Lord of all, **to you we pray.**

Ascended Lord, it is you who we see as Lord, not the government, not the City, not big business, not the media or Silicon Valley. We pray that through the values and beliefs of faithful men and women, you will establish a culture of integrity, truthfulness and compassion in all of society's institutions. So may we declare with ever-greater confidence that Jesus is Lord.

Lord of all, **to you we pray.**

Ascended Lord, we see a world of beauty and tragedy, the wonderful wreckage of Eden. We pray that your ways of peace and justice may increasingly sideline the ways of violence and contempt. We pray particularly for your ways to prevail in . . . *(places in the news)*. Bless the work of the United Nations and establish a common passion for justice and the gift of hope.

Lord of all, **to you we pray.**

Ascended Lord, we know you are Lord of the Church but sometimes the evidence is thin. We try to be the Church in our own strength, with our own wisdom, and so end up trading prejudices for truth and manipulation for compassion. We pray that we may again be enchanted by the gospel and inspired by the vision of a Church transformed through love – starting here, now, with us.

Lord of all, **to you we pray.**

Ascended Lord, as we look ahead at the coming week we pray that in every part of our lives – at work, at play, in our relationships, with our money, our time and our temptations – you will be Lord. In silence now we offer you this week . . .

Lord of all, **to you we pray.**

(29) PENTECOST 1

A possible verse and response would be: 'Come, Holy Spirit, and renew us in your service.'

God of Spirit and power, you fell upon the disciples that first Pentecost, warm as a smile and quick as a lightning strike. Teach us that what happened *out* there and *back* then can happen *in* here and *right* now. We too can know your power in our lives, but only as the power of love. Open us, we pray, to that same power of love which alone changes lives.

Come, Holy Spirit, **and renew us in your service.**

God of Spirit and truth, give us such confidence in the truth of the gospel that we're happy to share our faith as naturally as the sun rises and a child plays. May your Spirit break open our reticence as it did the fear of the disciples on that first day of Pentecost. And may our lives tell the same story as our lips.

Come, Holy Spirit, **and renew us in your service.**

God of Spirit and creativity, bless the creative pursuits of your people – the artists and musicians, the poets and writers, the dramatists, sculptors and graphic designers, the potters and film-makers and all in creative industries. Bless us too as we create on a lesser scale, tend our gardens, take our photographs, cook our signature dishes. May the Spirit find us willing co-workers in the creation of all things authentic and beautiful.

Come, Holy Spirit, **and renew us in your service.**

God of Spirit and community, this is the day the Church was born. We know the Church is still in draft form; you want so much more for us. May your Spirit mould us into the likeness of Jesus so that we live the way he lived and love the way he loved. And all in the fellowship of his body, the Church.

Come, Holy Spirit, **and renew us in your service.**

God of Spirit and joy, melt the frost around our hearts and fill us with the warmth of Pentecost. Search us with your Spirit until faith is burned into our lives and we dare to live differently. Save us from conventional faith and send us out to live and work, led by the Spirit, to your praise and glory.

(30) PENTECOST 2

This verse and response could be used: 'God of Pentecost, fill us afresh with your Spirit.'

On that morning of Pentecost there was a sound like a mighty wind, rushing through the room where the disciples were gathered. Lord God, we sometimes forget that you are powerful. Forgive us for limiting you to the small size of our imaginations, thinking of you as a God without thunder. May we offer to the world a God without limits, an infinite source of love, creativity and wisdom. We pray for courage to be reticent in what we claim to know about you but confident in how we trust in you.

God of Pentecost, **fill us afresh with your Spirit.**

On that morning of Pentecost tongues of fire appeared to rest on each of the disciples – a divine fire that spoke of holiness and the blazing presence of God. We may not expect fire every day, but we pray, gracious Spirit, for an awareness of your presence in the midst of everyday things. May we not seal up our expectation of you in special buildings but encounter you at work wherever we choose to notice, in home and workplace, in shared meals and acts of love, in nature and works of art. Keep us alert to the holy fire that energizes all of life, glowing beneath the surface of everything.

God of Pentecost, **fill us afresh with your Spirit.**

On that morning of Pentecost the disciples spoke in other languages, causing amazement and perplexity. Gracious Spirit, help us to speak in the language of love, however we express it. We pray for our church, that the language people hear from us may be one that affirms and encourages, welcomes and inspires, comforts and forgives. As we look ahead at this week and the things we will be doing, help us to see that our body language must match our speech, for we will be judged by what we actually do, rather than by what we think.

God of Pentecost, **fill us afresh with your Spirit.**

On that morning of Pentecost many people turned to you and became part of the family of believers. Gracious God, you know how much we would love more people to become part of your family here. Give us confidence, we pray, not in our latest schemes but in your good Spirit, blowing like the wind wherever it will. Make us concerned not to be successful but to be faithful, and to let you give the increase in your own time and your own way. But here we are bold to pray for your Spirit to touch the lives of some we know whom we would love to encounter you, and we name them in our hearts now . . .

God of Pentecost, **fill us afresh with your Spirit.**

On *this* morning of Pentecost, gracious God, we pray that you will flow afresh into our lives and fill us with *your* life. And what we say of you in our creeds may we believe in our hearts and demonstrate in lives filled with the abundance of your Spirit.

(31) TRINITY SUNDAY

A possible verse and response could be: 'God the Holy Trinity, make us strong in faith and love.'

One theologian described the Trinity like this: God, Father, Son and Holy Spirit – greater than great, closer than close, more loving than love.

Holy Father, you are indeed greater than great, beyond our best attempts to imagine the depth of your mystery or the height of your transcendence. We try to understand, but words stagger and fall over. Hold us steady when we almost give up, or when the black crow of doubt flaps across our hearts. Show us again – for we forget – that at the heart of mystery and transcendence is love; love as the energy behind creation and the foundation of all life. May we build our lives on the firm foundation of your love – which is greater than great.

God the Holy Trinity, **make us strong in faith and love.**

Gracious Son of the Father, you are indeed closer than close. You know the scrapyard of the human heart, the sad tale of our addiction to ourselves. Thank you for blazing through human life and showing us how it could be done, how we could live well, with grace and generosity, justice and kindness. Help us to take all our life's bearings from you, to follow your path and be covered in your dust – the dust of our rabbi, who is closer than close.

God the Holy Trinity, **make us strong in faith and love.**

Good Spirit of the Father and the Son, you are indeed more loving than love. In you there is no evasion, only the true path of compassion for all people and all creation. We pray that you will blow through our lives, if necessary at hurricane force, until we grasp that our deepest calling, this and every day, is to love you and our neighbour, without reserve. Circle us, Lord, in the love which is closer than close, and enable us to circle others in it too.

68

God the Holy Trinity, **make us strong in faith and love.**

Greater than great, closer than close, more loving than love; we place in the strong hands of the Trinity the concerns of our hearts, the tasks of the week, the people we love, the fears we hide, the world and its labours and all things living. We pray in silence now for these our own particular concerns . . .

God the Holy Trinity, **make us strong in faith and love.**

5 SPECIAL SUNDAYS

(32) NEW YEAR

A familiar verse and response could be used.

Lord of the years, you who see beyond the bend of time, we approach the new year with both hope and anxiety. Until the year gets properly established it feels fragile and new-born. We pray that you will settle and strengthen our hearts as we entrust this year to you, and ask you to fill it with depth and discovery. May it truly be the Year of Our Lord, 20 . . *(date)*.

Lord of the years, our world order feels to be in constant flux and we sometimes wonder whether the centre can hold. We pray for our political leaders and their international counterparts, men and women with much the same gifts and insecurities as anyone else, but carrying great responsibilities. Give them vision, but keep them grounded. Give them wisdom and save them from pride. May their opinions and decisions be well informed and rooted in a desire for justice and peace. Especially at the start of this year we pray for . . . *(current world issues)*.

Lord of the years, we would love this year to be a good one for the poor and unregarded, those for whom you have a special care. Hundreds of millions live on less than £1 a day, without access to the basics – clean water, proper housing, healthcare, education, work that pays adequately. We pray for the re-ordering of our priorities to be in line with those of Jesus. May we see the poor with the eyes of Jesus, and see Jesus in the eyes of the poor. We pray in particular for these troubled areas . . . *(current places of hunger and need)*.

Lord of the years, as we stand at the gate of the year you know what goes on in the confused and troubled pathways of our minds and hearts. We want the best but fear the worst, and are not sure whether we can trust either ourselves or others. So we turn again towards the light that streams from the crib, the cross and the empty tomb. In your light may we see light. In your light may we rest secure.

Lord of the years, we start this year with glad and clear intent, expressed in the words of the Methodist Covenant which, if we will, we can echo in our hearts:

Gracious God, I am no longer my own, but yours. Put me to what you will, rank me with whom you will. Put me to doing, put me to suffering: let me be employed for you, or laid aside for you: exalted for you or brought low for you: let me be full, let me be empty: let me have all things, let me have nothing: I freely and wholeheartedly yield all things to your pleasure and disposal. And now, glorious and blessed God, Father, Son and Holy Spirit, you are mine and I am yours, so be it. And the covenant now made on earth, let it be ratified in heaven.

Amen and amen.

(33) MOTHERING SUNDAY

Care is needed on this day. Not everyone has had a good experience of mothering, and others would love to be mothers but it's not been possible. We need to think around our congregation and be sensitive to who will be there. We need to remember also that we don't know the secrets of everyone's heart . . .

One of the normal responses might be used after each section: 'Lord, in your mercy . . . ' or 'Lord, hear us . . . '

Gracious God, giver of all good gifts and giver of all good mothering, we thank you for the mothering we have received, the security, the cherishing, the encouragement, the thousand practicalities of motherhood. 'Thank you' is too small a word, but thank you to them and to you.

Gracious God, we recognize the demands of mothering, the provision of everything, the giving and forgiving, the necessary worrying, the perpetual chasing up, the endless clearing up. We pray for all mothers, that the well of generous loving may daily be refilled from the deep well of your endless love.

Gracious God, we pray for those for whom becoming a mother has proved impossible. Come close in that monthly disappointment. Hold all such couples in your tender embrace, you who in the life and death of Jesus showed yourself to be not so much almighty as all-vulnerable.

We pray for mothers for whom the task is a particular struggle – to put the right food on the table, to make ends meet, to deal with hyperactive children, to do everything and still be available to listen. Help the rest of us to be discerning and supportive of such families. May our churches be places of care and support; of play, peace and perspective for all parents.

Gracious God, we recognize that sometimes good mothering fails. People are stretched too far or they bring to the task of mothering too many wounds of their own. Where damage has been done to them, enable such mothers to find grace to forgive the past and to offer a different type of mothering themselves.

Gracious God, thank you for your mothering and fathering of all creation. All things exist *from* you; all people are loved *by* you; all families are blessed *in* you. May our human loving reflect, however faintly, your boundless, infinite loving, until we all come, gladly, to our eternal home in Christ our Lord.

(34) FATHERS' DAY

Once Mothering Sunday had become Mothers' Day in the public mind it was inevitable that Fathers' Day would soon follow, and so it has. The Church has been slower in catching up with the public mood but it would be good to focus on the vital tasks of fathering as well. As with Mothering Sunday, care needs to be taken to allow for a range of experiences of fathering in the congregation.

One of the usual verses and responses could be used: 'Lord, in your mercy . . . ' or 'Lord, hear us . . . '

Good and loving God, we are glad to give thanks for the love and dedication of the vast majority of fathers in the joyful task of bringing up children. Thank you for the time they give to work in the house and play in the garden, and to offering their children a model of committed care. Where fathers feel unsure or inadequate, reassure them that undiluted love is sufficient. Give them patience when things go wrong or get broken, and a reminder that lives are shaped over years, not fixed in minutes.

Good and loving God, we pray for those fathers who, like many mothers also, struggle to balance home and work responsibilities. Give both parents patient understanding and grace, both with each other and with their children. We pray too for those fathers who are separated by divorce from their children's day-to-day lives and miss them deeply. May their hearts be both tender in love and guarded from pain as they seek to redeem a less-than-perfect situation.

Good and loving God, we are glad to know you as Father, while acknowledging the gains of knowing you also through the image of Mother, for you are beyond gender. Show us how to parent our children richly and imaginatively, to offer them a creative mix of freedom within a secure framework to stimulate their minds, cherish their ideas, enjoy their mischief, encourage their curiosity, guard their vulnerability, and to love them, love them, love them.

Good and loving God, we pray for fathers across the world struggling to be good fathers when they can't give their children sufficient food and shelter, security and education. Save them from despair. Give the international community a continued determination to eradicate poverty, control disease and bring down infant mortality. And make us agents in the answering of our own prayers.

Good and loving God, who gave Joseph to be a good and loving father to your Son Jesus, make ours a *world* of good and loving fathers, for Jesus' sake and the sake of our children.

(35) HARVEST

*These intercessions could be made more vivid in some less formal
Harvest Festivals if a bag of shopping is used as a visual aid. Care
needs to be taken that this doesn't come across as cringeworthy.*

It's harvest. Imagine you've just come back from the supermarket
with bags full of shopping that now need to be put away. First
out of the bags – milk.

Generous God, we thank you for the dairy farmers who make
sure we always have milk available, whatever the conditions.
They have early starts and miserable weather, and sometimes the
price they get is lower than the cost of production. Bless them,
Lord, for their patience and faithfulness. And bless those cows
too, solemnly yielding their milk for our health and well-being.

For what we have received, **make us truly thankful.**

Next out of the shopping bag – fruit: apples, bananas, oranges.
Thank you, generous God, for the fruits of the earth produced
beautifully and abundantly through the grace of nature, the hard
work of the farmers, the skill of the transporters, the investment
of the wholesalers and the purchasing power of the retailers.
May we never take for granted the appearance of fruit on the
supermarket shelves.

For what we have received, **make us truly thankful.**

Next out of the shopping bag – tea and coffee. Thank you,
generous God, for these staples of our daily life, hard won from
hillsides across the world, in India, Sri Lanka, Kenya, Brazil,
Indonesia and elsewhere. Protect the farmers, we pray, as they
face unpredictable weather and the volatility of the market. Make
us responsible, fair-trade consumers, aware that at the end of the
chain is a piece of land, a low-paid worker and a family to feed.

For what we have received, **make us truly thankful.**

Next out of the shopping bag – rice, staple diet of millions.
Remind us, good Lord, that while we in the north face an

76

epidemic of weight-gain and obesity, millions in the Global South go hungry. How can this be happening? Show us, Lord, the error of our ways; help us to be more than fair – to be generous – in sharing the world's extravagance. There is indeed enough for everyone's need, but not for our insatiable greed.

For what we have received, **make us truly thankful.**

Our shopping bags still bulge. Next time we go to the supermarket the shelves will again be overflowing and we'll have an astonishing choice of wonderful foodstuffs. We stand in awe before the abundance of the planet, year after year. 'As long as the earth endures, seedtime and harvest, cold and heat, summer and winter, day and night will never cease,' says the Lord.

For *all* that we have received, **make us truly thankful.**

(36) REMEMBRANCE SUNDAY

Care has to be taken on this day to fit in with the mood of the occasion but also to widen and deepen it. This intercession would suit some occasions and not others. A time of silence between each section should be longer than we usually dare – but not two minutes. Fifteen seconds might still seem a long time.

On Remembrance Sunday there's always two minutes' silence. Silence to remember the sacrifice *of* so many, *for* so many. We try to remember, but we weren't there in the two world wars. Instead we remember films we've watched and pictures we've seen. Give us, Lord, a glimpse of what it meant for so many to be afraid but still be brave, to want to live but be prepared to die. Give us imagination and empathy to crouch with them in the darkness, knowing the next few minutes could change, or end, their lives. Help us to remember.

Silence.

Two minutes' silence – for the sacrifice goes on. Men and women have fought and died, and been wounded and disabled, in war after war in recent years too. We give thanks and pray for the Royal British Legion, Help the Heroes and other service organizations in which people give their time and skill for survivors. We pray for those who now face a lifetime of disablement or post-traumatic stress disorder. Bless them with new horizons and different opportunities.

Silence.

Two minutes' silence. Silence to pray for nations to be at peace with each other. We know we have a choice: a world at peace or a world in pieces. And constantly we choose the latter. Give us, good Lord, a vision of a world at peace, and never let it fade away. Absorb and neutralize our hatreds in the arms of Jesus on the cross. Disarm us at the doorway to the empty tomb. May peace always be our goal and peace always be our method.

Silence.

Two minutes' silence. Silence for things too deep for words. Silence before a football match; silence after a national tragedy; silence before the grave of a loved one. Silence when words crumble and only silence can describe the pain. Lord, make us skilled at the use of silence in the face of loss, particularly remembering today . . . *(current experiences)*.

Silence.

Two minutes' silence. Silence to help us return to our still centre, the place where God is always present, awaiting our return. Lord, draw us back to that place where you are *real*, for we, so much of the time, are not. Make silence our friend.

Silence.

Two minutes' silence. To remember. And never to forget.

(37) BIBLE SUNDAY

*Every Sunday is Bible Sunday in the sense that the words of
Scripture will always be a core element of worship. So these
intercessions can be used at any time, although there is a Sunday
in the autumn which many churches keep as one to focus on the
Bible. A good verse and response would be: 'Your word is a lamp
to our feet and a light to our path.'*

The Bible is read by scholars, men and women of wisdom and
skill who help us understand this, the most popular – but often
unread – book in the world. God of the life-giving word, give our
scholars skill and insight to unearth the treasures of the Bible and
enrich our appreciation of it.

Your word is a lamp to our feet **and a light to our path.**

The Bible is read by ministers, men and women who care
about Scripture and want it to transform people's lives. God
of the life-giving word, give our ministers patience to unpack
the meaning of Bible passages week by week in ways that
communicate fresh wisdom for our daily living.

Your word is a lamp to our feet **and a light to our path.**

The Bible is read by students, young men and women wanting to
make sense of life and to find something that holds it all together.
God of the life-giving word, give our students clear vision to
see that the Bible is a glorious love story in which you pursue
your wayward people with endless patience to give us back our
birthright: life in abundance.

Your word is a lamp to our feet **and a light to our path.**

The Bible is read by men and women under pressure at work
and at home, trying to find the best way to live in a noisy,
distracted world. God of the life-giving word, give to this stressed
generation grace to hear Scripture's invitation to be part of the
eternal conversation between heaven and earth, and in those
words to find peace and inspiration.

Your word is a lamp to our feet **and a light to our path.**

The Bible is read by people in prison, often lonely, lost and in quiet despair. God of the life-giving word, help them to hear the freedom song that rings through the Bible, telling us that there is liberty for captives and hope for us all.

Your word is a lamp to our feet **and a light to our path.**

The Bible is read by people, ordinary people, everywhere in the world, over two billion of us and more every day. God of the life-giving word, help us all to read the Bible with head, heart and hands – head to grapple with it, heart to love you through it, and hands to obey your call to action within it.

So may your word *for ever* be a lamp to our feet **and a light to our path.**

(38) DEDICATION FESTIVAL

This is the day on which a church celebrates the anniversary of it being dedicated as a house of prayer. It isn't the day that celebrates the saint to which the church is dedicated – such days are obviously dispersed throughout the year and different intercessions would apply to different saints. Watch for some of the assumptions of these prayers – they might need adapting.

God of both old stones and us your living stones, we thank you for this holy ground that carries the sacred memories of so many people – of baptisms, weddings and funerals, Midnight Masses, Royal Jubilees and prayers in time of war. Tears of joy and sorrow, prayers of hope and anguish, deep-felt promises and anxious bargains – all these have soaked into the stones. Thank you for the musty smell of old stone, damp prayer books and last week's flowers. Thank you for the way our church has kept watch over the streets by night, and week by week echoed the angels' song of praise.

May this be a temple of your presence, **a place of your glory on earth.**

God of past, present and future, thank you for the affection of the community for this place, rooted in holy history but resting on another foundation and bearing witness to another King. May this place speak with quiet eloquence of a kingdom where everyone lives under your blessing and where Christians seek to be a blessing to others. Keep us coming here to sustain the vision of a community transformed, at peace, creative and united.

May this be a temple of your presence, **a place of your glory on earth.**

God of warmth and welcome, thank you for a place where people can slow down and loiter and be at ease with you. Thank you for space, silence and simplicity. And when the place is empty, thank you for the angels crowding the rafters and folding their wings to settle in the pews. Help us to keep our churches open and welcoming, making space for dreams and soaking up anxieties. But give us imagination also to use our churches for community activities, for concerts and feasts, markets and meetings, lunch clubs and holiday weeks. Encourage us to be generous with our special places, in the spirit of the One who said that the Sabbath was made for humankind, not humankind for the Sabbath.

May this be a temple of your presence, **a place of your glory on earth.**

God of the old stones and the living stones, keep us from thinking that our church is a building when really it's a people. Keep us from the easy slide into worship of an idol, a building that delights the heart but doesn't change the way we think or live. Give us the spiritual freedom to be a pilgrim people, ever ready to travel on, to leave behind the settled places with their comfortable familiarity. May we always seek a kingdom which is yet to come.

May this be a temple of your presence, **a place of your glory on earth.**

Bless us, we pray, as we, the living stones, celebrate the old stones, in the name of the Cornerstone, Jesus Christ our Lord.

6 THEMES

(39) THE CHURCH HERE AND EVERYWHERE

This intercession starts with the local and moves outward, raising our sights to the global Church. Much local colour can be added. A familiar response could be used.

Lord of the Church, thank you for this church – the place, the people, the history and what it's meant to generations of people living near. Thank you for the people who have flowed in and out through the doors, faithful or searching, joyful or sad, hopeful or anxious. Thank you for the part this church has played in the lives of so many and the way the love of God has been made known in worship and service of others.

Lord of the Church, we pray for the churches near us, all with their own treasured story *(name some of them)*. We pray for their well-being and for creative relationships across the network of local churches, each centred on Christ and longing to make him known. In particular we pray for . . . *(local initiatives taken together)*.

Lord of the Church, we give thanks that across the country churches stand as great Post-it notes, reminding people of your presence in their midst. There are church towers punching the sky and church spires piercing the horizon. Churches give soul to every community, and without them there's a vacuum in the centre of community life. Enable us to keep our churches open and available, flexible and forward-looking – sacraments of your love as outward and visible signs of your inward, invisible grace.

Lord of the Church, across Europe there are enormous numbers of churches speaking of the Christian heritage that gave birth to the institutions of government, the legal system, hospitals, schools, the arts, philanthropy and so much more. Help our continent not to renege on its past but to value its heritage as a springboard to an ever more just, peaceful and compassionate future. Especially we pray for . . . *(current issues)*.

Lord of the Church, across the world the centre of gravity for Christianity has moved south. Thank you for the huge growth in the worldwide Church – 70,000 more Christians every day. Thank you for the variety of expression in worship and church life, in mission, ministry and social engagement. We pray especially for the links we have in . . . Bless our brothers and sisters, and strengthen our fellowship with them.

Lord of the Church, from here to there, from *(this church)* to *(a far distant church)*, we all belong to you; we have all heard your call, left our nets and followed you. We are not yet what we should be, but we are not stuck. Shape us into the Church you want us to become, to the glory of the Father, in the power of the Spirit and in union with Christ.

(40) SILENCE

These intercessions can be used at any time, and particularly if a congregation is wanting to explore a quieter spirituality. In a noisy world the Church may have a special vocation to help people reclaim the inner stillness essential to human well-being. These intercessions need space and silence – if anything, reduce the number of words!

Silent God, forgive our noisy world. Forgive the way we avoid deep things by filling our lives promiscuously with words, music, activity, speed – anything, indeed, that disguises our need for stillness and space. Help us to be quiet so that in going deep we may meet your gracious Spirit who longs to heal our fragmented souls. Help us to value silence, to experiment with it and eventually to love it, because we're beginning to hear the whisper of your gentle voice.

Silence for reflection.

Silent God, let us not confuse your silence with absence or inactivity. In silence you gave birth to creation, to Jesus, to salvation, to resurrection. You are not a noisy God but we are noisy people, apparently needing more and more distraction from our emptiness. Take away our fear of silence. Enable us to hear the soul music beneath the surface noise and to explore the meaning of that music, the love song you have sung to us for ever.

Silence for reflection.

Silent God, the world is chaotic, in part because it's forgotten how to be still. Nations defend themselves and attack others with words, speeches, media statements, inspections, commissions, reports, arguments. We give no space to the still, small voice that alone gives wisdom and makes peace. We speak too much, too soon and too long. Quieten the anger of nations, we pray; slow them down, help them to say less and listen more. In silence we pray for particular places where words of intolerance and hatred have led to actions of violence and destruction . . .

Silence for reflection.

Silent God, if we can be quiet, silence will prevent us trying to possess other people and fit them into our needs and desires. Silence will set them free to be themselves with us, and us with them. Then we can meet honestly and truthfully. Help us to be quietly attentive to each person we meet this week, to empty ourselves of the desire to control, and to listen to them and to you. We think now of those we know we'll spend time with this week, and we offer them, unconditionally, to you . . .

Silence for reflection.

Thank you, Lord, for your silence. Make us more like you.

(41) WORK

A familiar response could be used.

Gracious God, you who never cease working to shape the kingdom in our midst, we pray for the world of work which we so often ignore in the life of the Church.

We pray for young people approaching paid employment for the first time, straight from school, college or university. The world of work may look exciting or daunting, welcoming or elusive, as they survey the bewildering possibilities of the future. So, we pray, give these young people peace of heart and determination of spirit as they pursue the jobs that will set them on their path through life. May employers see through nervousness or over-confidence to the true potential that lies within each young person.

We pray for our fellow citizens caught up in the heat and pressures of work. May we and they be honest and true, loyal and industrious, bringing our best qualities to bear on our various tasks. We pray particularly for Christians faced with ethical dilemmas at work but wanting to integrate their faith with their working life. Give them strength of character and the wisdom that comes from the mind of Christ.

We pray for those who are out of work and feeling the insecurity, the loss of identity and even perhaps the despair that sometimes goes with unemployment. Help them to reach further into their real identity and there find a deeper confidence that they are created, valued and loved just for themselves. Give them grit and hope as they pursue different ways forward, and supportive family and friends to go on the journey with them.

We pray for those who have retired, often with a mixture of emotions – relief and expectation, but also loss and bewilderment. Teach us all that 'being' is as important as 'doing' and that new forms of both being and doing are always possible; that life never ceases to be an adventure and that your ample resources are always only a prayer away.

Gracious God, ever present and sustaining your creation, thank you for enlisting us as co-workers in your great project of bringing to life a new creation in our midst. Your kingdom come *on earth*, as it is in heaven. Let it come, Lord; let it come.

(42) LIGHT

Light is obviously a strong Christian theme and this set of intercessions could apply to many seasons, such as Advent, Christmas, Candlemas or any Sunday when it feels as if a dose of light would encourage the church in its life and prayer. Most of what comes below is bidding, and the prayer will be in the silence offered at the end of the bidding. That silence therefore needs to be long enough for people really to pray. Then a simple verse and response could be: 'God is light, and in him is no darkness at all.'

We are told by John in his first letter that 'God is light, and in him is no darkness at all'. Imagine, then, that the light of God shines like a blazing fire in the heart of our prayers, and illuminates different needs in the world around us. The light is unquenchable, inexhaustible; it shines in the darkness and the darkness can never overcome it.

God is light, **and in him is no darkness at all.**

Let that light shine first on people close to you – your family and closest friends, those for whom you care deeply and whose needs you know. Pray that the light of God may shine on them, on their questions, confusions and hidden needs. On their health, their hopes, their values and beliefs. Pray for them now, that God will fill them with light . . .

God is light, **and in him is no darkness at all.**

Let the light of God shine now on any people or place that's been in the news this week and that's caught your attention and awakened your concern. It could be . . . or . . . or even . . . Pray for those people or that place in all the complexity that makes it so hard to sort out. Hold that situation open to God, so that the light of God may shine on it and fill it with light. Pray in silence now . . .

God is light, **and in him is no darkness at all.**

Let the light of God shine now on this church [or group]. We try
to follow Christ, but so often our love is intermittent and we fail
to demonstrate the life-changing compassion of Jesus. In your
mind's eye see the light of God filling this church, chasing away
the dark corners, pouring light into every act of worship and
every act of love. See the light of God filling the people around
you with faith, hope and love. See it happening now; pray for it,
a people filled with light . . .

God is light, **and in him is no darkness at all.**

Gracious God, you have given us a light to lighten the Gentile
in all of us. May we be open to your light this week. May we be
people of light who walk in the light and reflect the light wherever
we go. We know it's a tall order to live like that, but we know
you're a God of infinite grace. Let light shine in our darkness and
show us a better way.

God is light, **and in him is no darkness at all.**

(43) FRIENDS

A possible verse and response would be: 'I do not call you servants any longer; **I call you friends.**'

Loving Father, we thank you for the way Jesus called his disciples friends and we delight in the privilege of sharing that relationship. As friends of Jesus, gathered here today, make us more aware of what that friendship means – that we are valued, trusted, even *enjoyed* for who we are – but also that we need to spend time with you, that we must not be too busy to pray, to loiter with you at odd points through the day. Help us not to miss the joy of your friendship. For Jesus said:

I do not call you servants any longer; **I call you friends.**

You call us friends and we would love to share that friendship with others. Or would we? It doesn't seem so from the way we rarely speak of it to others. Help us to be more natural in talking of the place of faith in our lives. Make us more relaxed and at ease in telling our story, or the bit of it that might help someone else. Make us talkative believers.

I do not call you servants any longer; **I call you friends.**

Thank you for the friends you have given us. We probably don't pray for them as much as we should and yet prayer is the best way we have of caring for anyone – placing them in your hands. Make us better friends, more patient, giving, forgiving, generous friends. Make us more like the friend that Jesus was to his friends, loving to the very end. We pray now for one or two special friends, holding them gratefully and hopefully before you . . .

I do not call you servants any longer; **I call you friends.**

We pray for those who have few friends, even no *real* friends who would stand by them whatever. Many are lonely in our overcrowded cities, and loneliness destroys people – their enjoyment of life, their hope, their health. We often give out our friendship in spoonfuls; instead, Lord, make us profligate in friendship, open in welcome, unprotected in love. Jesus, friend of all on the margins, enlist us as friends of the friendless. As they come to mind, we pray for any we know now . . .

I do not call you servants any longer; **I call you friends.**

Loving Father, we know we should be more of a friend to the earth on which we depend. We know that nature, like people, can be exhausted, and it can't be properly re-stocked. We pray for those who abuse the friendship of the earth, taking without giving. May we repent of society's rampant consumerism; all we need is less. We pray for governments, that they'll keep to the agreements they've made to lower carbon emissions and honour our common home . . .

I do not call you servants any longer; **I call you friends.**

The last words of Gregory of Nyssa were, 'The one thing that's truly important is becoming God's friend.' Lord, make us better friends, to you, to each other, to the friendless and to the earth. Because Jesus said:

I do not call you servants any longer; **I call you friends.**

(44) RELATIONSHIPS

Relationships offer our most important and meaningful experiences, though they can also be very painful. Each of us is at the heart of a web of relationships which we might well bring to God in intercession. A possible verse and response would be: 'Those who live in love, live in God; and God lives in them.'

Loving God, we thank you for the relationships that feed grace into our lives, the people we can rely on implicitly, who love us and cheer us on, but who love us too much not to be honest. May we return love for love, life for life, and cherish those very special close relationships.

Those who live in love, live in God; **and God lives in them.**

Loving God, we pray for those who are struggling with key relationships, especially for those relationships where love seems to have lost the will to live. Give them grace to renew the relationship or, if necessary, grace to fail – for you always desire love that lives, not love that has died. Please comfort, heal, restore or release – whatever is best and true. We pray for any people we know who are caught up in this struggle . . .

Those who live in love, live in God; **and God lives in them.**

Loving God, open our hearts to new relationships and friendships. Prevent us from turning inward and cultivating only what's familiar and comfortable. Help us to receive everyone we meet as Christ, and to enjoy the richness of other lives and stories. Help us to set aside prejudice and see Jesus in every neighbour. We look ahead at the coming week and the people we're likely to meet . . . .

Those who live in love, live in God; **and God lives in them.**

Loving God, you have made us to live together in community. No one is an island, entire of itself: we are all 'a piece of the continent, a part of the main'. We pray for the community in which we are set physically, and the various communities of which we personally are a part. May our church not only be 'a part of the main' but a key player in shaping a community of mutual respect, service and creativity. In all we say and do, make us a community of grace.

Those who live in love, live in God; **and God lives in them.**

Loving God, build your community here, strong and true, on the rock of Christ. May our roots go down so that our walls may come down too, and we can welcome all you give us, in the name of Jesus Christ our Lord.

(45) HEALTH

We are all concerned about health – our own, the health of others and the nation's health services. Instead of focusing just on a list of people who are sick, this intercession broadens out into wider health issues. Any, or no, response can be used between sections.

God of health and wholeness, we thank you for the ministry of Jesus to the sick, demonstrating that you want us to be well enough to live the abundant life your Son promised. Give us a balanced understanding of our own health, not obsessing about aches and pains, but bringing to you our real needs and the needs of others who are in genuine distress, among them . . . *(names)*.

God of health and wholeness, we think with gratitude of the skill and dedication of consultants, doctors, nurses, GPs and health visitors. But we pray also for the army of other health professionals – managers, researchers, technicians, porters, ambulance crews, cleaners and cooks – that they may be sustained, rewarded and encouraged in the tasks they undertake. We bring to mind and pray for any we know who occupy these roles . . .

God of health and wholeness, we know that mental illness destroys the lives of some people and causes others to limp through life. Thank you for those who work in this field of often entrenched mental illness. Give them patience, and enable them to see the deep value of every human life. In our prayers now perhaps we could see Jesus coming alongside anyone we know who's suffering from depression or other mental illness, remembering that Jesus had a particular concern for those who experienced this kind of oppression. See him there, with that person, now. What does he do? . . . *(longer pause)*

God of health and wholeness, we know that our well-being depends not only on the functioning of the body but on a host of emotional and social factors. So we pray that we may offer generously to others the gifts of friendship, kindness and community. May we identify social needs in our neighbourhood and try to meet them. May we exercise our responsibilities as citizens both of our earthly community and of the kingdom of heaven, bringing the light and life of Christ to any and all people in our neighbourhood. This week make us alert to the possibility of making a difference in some way, to somebody.

God of health and wholeness, thank you for the miracle of our minds and bodies. May we treasure them, respect them and offer them to your service, through Jesus Christ our Healer and Lord.

(46) WHOLENESS AND SICKNESS

Here is another intercession on the theme of health – a theme familiar to all churchgoers and vital to us all. There are so many dimensions to this theme and it's important not to reduce it to a weekly list of the sick. A familiar response could be used.

Gracious God, we give thanks for the miracle of the human body, so integrated and so clever at repairing itself. We give thanks for the bodies that have been our best friends for so long. And we give thanks for our amazing health service, restoring the healthy working of our bodies and giving us back the freedoms we thought we had lost. We pray for the huge variety of contributors to our national health service, from managers, porters and secretaries to consultants, nurses and physios, from GPs and district nurses to paramedics and ambulance crews. Bless them with fair reward and rich fulfilment as they work for our well-being.

Gracious God, we pray for the complex interplay between hospital services and community-based social care. When people fall down the cracks between the two, may there be fresh thinking and new resources. May a person never be a number, nor a patient a problem, for all are made in your image and all are the recipients of your love.

Gracious God, we pray for those who are trapped in the trauma of long-term suffering or slow terminal decline. We think of the devastation of motor neurone disease, multiple sclerosis, dementia and various forms of cancer, of people with quadriplegia and locked-in syndrome – and many others. Make clear to us all that when the body retreats, your love remains; when the physical closes down, your grace and peace go deeper still. We bring to you in prayer particular people for whom we have a special care . . .

Gracious God, we give thanks for the patient ministry of hospices and home-based palliative care teams. Thank you for the precious gifts they bring to so many families faced with situations where

98

they feel out of their depth. We pray for our own local hospice, for the work being done there this very day . . .

Gracious God, all of us carry a number of suffering people in our hearts, and as a church we carry many more. As we pray for them now, we reach out to them in love, knowing that you will use our love for their benefit. These, then, are the people we bring to you . . . *(church list or space for personal prayer)*. Give to each the peace, light and healing of your loving presence.

And for ourselves too, Lord, we pray. Jesus said to the blind man by the roadside in Jericho, 'What do you want me to do for you?' May we be brave enough to tell him now . . .

(47) DEATH

*The Great Pretender, death, holds humanity in thrall and
we spend huge amounts of time and effort trying to avoid it.
Christians, of all people, can look death in the eye and whisper
another word – resurrection. It's good if we can pray realistically
about death, and this intercession could therefore be used at any
time, but particularly around All Souls' Day, or when death is
in the air after, say, a royal death. A familiar response could be
used.*

Lord of life and death, we know that death has a 100 per cent
success rate. It's guaranteed. Help us to be comfortable with this
fact and to know that, whenever and however it comes, you will
be present all the way. Knowing neither the time nor the manner
of our death, help us to commit ourselves wholeheartedly to
you, living life to the full, in complete trust in your kindness and
goodness towards us.

Lord of life and death, we pray for the few we know, and the
many we don't know, who are now having to face the full
bewilderment of bereavement – the regrets, the stabs of memory,
the aching absence. Help them to find their own way and to
resist the blueprints and kindly advice of others. May they know
it's OK to feel as they do. May they be kind to themselves and
only do what they can manage. We hold before you now . . .
*(either church list, well-known person or space for personal
remembrance).*

Lord of life and death, we pray particularly for those who have
experienced sudden death in their family in a way that's left them
stunned. There are victims of road accidents, accidents at work,
operations that go wrong, heart attacks in the middle of normal
days. The morning routine, people rushing through the bathroom,
grabbing breakfast, shouting farewell; the front door slams – for
ever. We pray that you will be especially close to these families,
broken in spirit, struggling to stand. Be their rock, their strong
tower, the One they can lean on. And give them a glimpse of a

new way, a half-open door into the future. If there are any we know, we pray for them now . . .

Lord of life and death, we live in a society desperately averse to death, denying it, resisting it, pushing it away by whatever means. Help us to be a society more at ease with death, more prepared to see it as the fulfilment of life, a final home rather than an enemy. We commend to your keeping the work of hospices and palliative care teams, Marie Curie and Macmillan support staff and many others who care quietly for loved ones in their homes. Bless them as they make dying as comfortable as possible – as they make dying normal.

Lord of life and death, help us as Christians to speak gently and graciously of our hope and trust in a risen Christ. May our care for others and our confidence in you bring peace and hope to troubled hearts. And may our lives proclaim what we believe:

'Alleluia, Christ is risen. **He is risen indeed, alleluia!**'

(48) STORM

These intercessions might fit a service when the country has
suffered a major storm and the consequences are all over our
screens. As ever, these intercessions are only a starter, to be used
as a springboard for something better and more local. 'Storm' is
also used here as a metaphor for many other issues and crises. A
possible verse and response would be: 'In you, O Lord, do we put
our trust. Save us and help us, Lord, we pray.'

Lord God, the storm has done/is doing great damage and people
are struggling in . . . We pray for hard-pressed victims pushed
to the edge and well-trained rescue services working round the
clock. As our weather becomes increasingly erratic, we pray
with penitence for a deeper respect for the earth and its delicate
weather systems. Where we are at fault with our addiction to
carbon consumption, Father, forgive us and change our hearts.

In you, O Lord, do we put our trust. **Save us and help us, Lord,**
we pray.

Lord God, many nations are caught up in storms of violence and
destruction. We think of . . . We look on from the relative security
of our country and wonder how it can have come to this, that men
and women still demonstrate such hatred and cruelty to each other.
We pray for every peacemaking initiative of the United Nations, and
for all people with peace in their hearts. Increase their determination
and strengthen their skill, until the storms of war are past.

In you, O Lord, do we put our trust. **Save us and help us, Lord,**
we pray.

Lord God, there are many people who this week are experiencing
storms of their own – of ill-health, of sudden injury, of their
world falling apart. In the heart of these storms, just as Jesus
brought peace to his disciples in a storm, hold these people close
in your strong presence and let your peace undergird their lives.
We pray for any we know, that your peace may go deep, and ever
deeper, into the heart of the storm . . .

In you, O Lord, do we put our trust. **Save us and help us, Lord, we pray.**

Lord God, the storms of life, physical and personal, destroy the settled fabric of our existence. Only you have the capacity to contain, heal and restore that fabric. Be present at the heart of our storms, we pray, and give us your peace.

In you, O Lord, do we put our trust. **Save us and help us, Lord, we pray.**

(49) LOSS

We all experience loss in various forms all our lives, but the only loss we usually mention in our intercessions is the loss of loved ones through death. In these intercessions we start there but broaden out; as such, they could be used at All Souls' or at other points in the year. A familiar verse and response could be used.

Gracious and loving God, week by week we bring to you the names of loved ones who have died and gone beyond us into eternal day. We recite the names, briefly remember and quickly move on. But to someone each life was, and remains, precious beyond telling. Help us to remember with respect and to empathize with sincerity when these names are read to us. And help those who still lie in the no-man's land of grief to adjust to this new reality and move to a different place, nearer to you. These names we present to you now . . .

Gracious and loving God, you know our losses: the people we lose, the relationships that founder, the working life that ends, the body that lets us down, the dreams that die. Our memories both bless and burn, as we think of what was, what might have been and what will never be again. Teach us not to be afraid, for in this life there will always be imperfection and all our symphonies will be unfinished. Instead enable us, and all those we know who are experiencing loss today, to release our memories and dashed hopes into your capacious hands, and to hear again your promise: 'I will always love you and stay with you.'

Gracious and loving God, help us to accept the fact that our political hopes also contain losses and disappointments. A new government starts with high hopes of what it can do and sees those hopes chipped away *(as in . . .)*. A peace negotiation believes it can bring an end to violence by common sense and compromise, only to come up against the intransigence of human nature *(as in . . .)*. A humanitarian relief operation stumbles against logistical and political obstacles *(as in . . .)*. We could easily lose hope. So grant to us, Lord, and to all who love peace, an indomitable spirit and an irrepressible hope. We continue to pray with conviction and courage, 'Your kingdom come on earth, as it is in heaven.'

Gracious and loving God, thank you for the brilliance we see every day in the natural world, in human achievement and in special people. Help us to delight in what is good and beautiful and so put into perspective the losses we inevitably experience. We offer you our own lives and losses, our incomplete stories and disappointments, and pray that finally you will bring us to our true end and best beginning in the company of Jesus Christ, who knew both life and loss, but in whom the last word is always 'life'.

(50) SPORT

How often have you heard intercessions about sport? And yet sport is a national obsession and, for very many people, the focus of their leisure, if not their lives. If God is the God of everything, then such a major preoccupation of so many must be God's concern too. These intercessions might be particularly appropriate when major sporting events are taking place, such as the Olympics, the football or rugby World Cup, Wimbledon, an Ashes series, etc., but sport often hits the front page as well as the back page, so these prayers might fit at other times too. A familiar verse and response could be used.

God of life and energy, thank you for the joy of sport, whether we do it or watch it. We recognize what a hold it has over so many of us and delight in the exhilaration and release it gives. Thank you for the amazing capacity of the human body – the speed, strength and stamina it can achieve; the flexibility, grace and skill it can develop; and the lessons we can learn from the disciplines of training and from working fluently as a team. May we never take for granted the wonder of the human body and its capacity for giving us pleasure through sport.

God of life and energy, we know that sport carries risk of injury and sometimes catastrophic damage. We know also that risk is a necessary component of freedom. We pray for those who have suffered lasting incapacity through sport – rugby players, racing drivers, skiers, boxers, climbers. We pray too for those who bring high-level skills to repair the damage, and for those who care for them over long years. We pray that you will build other resurrections into their lives and sustain their love of sport.

God of life and energy, we confess that corruption in the use of drugs and the misuse of money creeps into sport as into so many institutions. We pray that you will disturb the consciences of perpetrators and strengthen the skills of regulators so that the high ideals of sport can be sustained and the original blessings of sport can be enjoyed. We pray for (*national and international sporting bodies in the news)*. In particular we pray for the young, for the purity of their pleasure in sport and the protection of their enthusiasm.

God of life and energy, many of us have favourite sports stars. The pressures on them are often huge, from the expectations of others as well as their own, and from the commercial and media circus that often surrounds them. So we pray now for one or two of our favourite sportspeople, for protection and integrity in the midst of those pressures, praying that they may be able to give of their best, and if possible achieve their dream. We name them in silence now . . .

Gracious and loving God, in the beauty, skill and grace of sporting achievement may we know your pleasure – and may the glory finally be yours.

(51) COMMUNITY

A familiar response could be used.

Gracious God, we thank you for those who freely give their
time and experience to lead and serve our communities. We
give thanks and pray for our parish, town, district and county
councillors and our town hall officers, often caught between
the needs of the community and the financial stringencies of
government funding. We also give thanks and pray for the
magistrates who stand in our place as fair and honest citizens
to administer justice. Bless those who lead and serve in these
valuable but vulnerable roles in civil society.

Gracious God, we give thanks and pray for those who create
community by setting up neighbourhood associations, youth
projects and heritage groups, walking clubs and book groups,
wine circles and sports clubs – and thousands more of those clubs
and groups that act as social glue in our local communities. May
we support and encourage all such local initiatives, and make our
contribution where we can. Teach us all, good Lord, how to build
community with whatever lies to hand, whether bricks of straw
or bricks of gold.

Gracious God, we pray particularly for communities that have
lost their way, left behind by dying industries, missing out
on regeneration funding and forgotten by the successful and
prosperous. Give to these communities the resilience, local
leadership and spirit of resurrection that they'll need if they're to
move on and thrive. May the partnership of the human spirit with
the Holy Spirit result in initiatives, business ventures and social
activities that will give shape and life to these communities.

Gracious God, you gave the Church to stand at the heart of
human communities, to be hubs of spiritual and social activity
committed to the flourishing of every neighbourhood. May
our churches be a blessing to the communities around them,
identifying their needs and talents, harnessing their energies and
celebrating their successes. As our churches sponsor and support

homeless projects and gardening clubs, children's groups and street pastors, dementia clubs and food banks, credit unions and lunch clubs, may the love of Christ be seen, shaped by the Spirit, to the glory of the Father. In this church we pray especially for . . .

Gracious God, thank you, as a Trinity of persons, Father, Son and Holy Spirit, for giving us a model of community, of mutual care and affirmation. May we on earth echo your life in heaven.

(52) MESS

We come to church looking like well-presented people with our lives sorted and the milk of human kindness as second nature. The reality is nearly always different because we all carry hurts, disappointments, complexities and failures. These intercessions try to be honest about this and put our compromised lives into a hopeful perspective. A familiar verse and response could be used.

God of mercy and grace, nothing is hidden from you. You know that our lives are often not as they seem on the surface, that underneath there's a lot of complexity and compromise where we struggle with the mess and battle with our demons. In fact our lives are often deep in the weeds and we stumble our way through as best we can. Lord, bless this mess, and assure us that what matters is honesty and good intent, not a happy, shiny surface. And that what matters above all is your love for us and your belief in us.

God of mercy and grace, the society we live in is messy too. We don't know how to solve the perennial problems of growing inequality, social care for the elderly, overcrowded prisons, an underachieving educational system, a wonderful NHS running out of money. Recall us, Lord, to fundamental values – to love of God and love of neighbour. Remind us that 'in quietness and in trust shall be our strength', not in noisy, assertive demands. Draw us into a deeper unity of purpose across our troubled social landscape. We pray in particular for *(area of life currently under pressure)* . . .

God of mercy and grace, our whole world should be declared unsafe. The threats to human flourishing multiply with the random brutality of terrorism, the warnings of climate catastrophe, the misery of refugees, the threat of cyber-attack and the nuclear ambition of rogue states. Help us, Lord, to hold out a clearer vision of a world living in conformity with the values of your kingdom, and which offers human dignity, equal worth and the enjoyment of political and cultural diversity. Keep offering us that vision, together with politicians who will work for it and institutions that embody it. We pray for . . . *(an area of current global threat in the news)*.

God of mercy and grace, we recognize that the mess of our world starts in the corkscrew of the human heart, our heart, and we alone are responsible for what happens there. Give us grace to clean out the dark corners and restore a sense of order and purpose. We know that this side of death we will always live with a degree of mess, but we ask for your continuing blessing as we attempt to love both our neighbours and ourselves, despite the problems. Bless us as we offer you now the week ahead . . .

Lord, in your mercy . . . **hear our prayer.**

(53) ANXIETY

It's often said that we live in an age of anxiety. People are scared of global events beyond their control and personal events that can undermine their lives. It can seem to many that we tread a delicate path through a landscape littered with landmines. But the most common phrase in the Bible is the injunction 'Do not be afraid'. These intercessions try to echo that reassurance. The three sections have the shape: bidding–prayer–refrain. The refrain could be spoken effectively by a second voice or as a congregational response.

We live in a world of threats, where the possibility of mutual destruction is ever with us and where new technologies are regularly giving nations new ways to destroy each other. We look across the globe and see threats in . . . and in . . . So much is beyond our control and could easily paralyse us.

God of peace, we pray for those who have responsibility for making and keeping peace: our world leaders, the UN Security Council, NATO, the European Union. Bless them with wisdom both human and divine as they navigate the paths of peace.

Hear the word of the Lord to his people: **'Do not be afraid, for I am with you.'**

Once we used to fight in the school playground, and now we fight in our marriages, workplaces and politics. We fight because we're afraid of being wrong, afraid of being found out, afraid of being beaten. And somehow we don't seem to know how to stop, how not to be afraid.

God of peace, we pray for any situation we know where people are caught in a web of conflict, distrust and fear. May they hear your words of reassurance and comfort as they test the paths of peace.

Hear the word of the Lord to his people: **'Do not be afraid, for I am with you.'**

We are good at disguising our anxieties, but our emotions are often much more fragile than they appear. People we know – or we ourselves – are trying to manage fears about hospital tests, personal debt, difficult relationships and more. Many people lack confidence in themselves and in their ability to cope. Many lives are crippled by low self-esteem and 'imposter syndrome'.

God of peace, we pray for ourselves and for others for whom these anxieties are daily companions. Give them and us the deeper assurance that nothing can separate us from your love, and that although we may be storm-tossed we will not be overcome.

Hear the word of the Lord to his people: **'Do not be afraid, for I am with you.'**

In silence now we bring to God any particular anxiety that we have at present, perhaps about the coming week, perhaps about a continuing situation in our lives. We bring them to the God of peace and hope . . . *(sufficient space for real prayer)*.

Hear the word of the Lord to his people: **'Do not be afraid, for I am with you.'**

(54) ENVIRONMENT

Ever-creating God, we would thank you daily for the beauty
and abundance of this world – if only we remembered. For it
is amazing. And yet the beauty of this planet is blemished and
its health is failing because we don't take proper care of it.
Instead we slash and burn the forests, pillage the land and hunt
animals to extinction. Why do we not weep, ashamed, ashamed?
Lord, revive our collective conscience and restore our sense of
responsible stewardship of the miracles of nature. Help us to
remember:

God saw everything that he had made, **and indeed, it was very
good.**

Ever-sustaining God, your good earth is gasping for breath as we
choke the atmosphere with carbon dioxide. Are we so in thrall to
the god of growth and the glittering prizes of a consumer culture
that we don't mind that the ship is sinking? Why do we not weep,
ashamed, ashamed? Lord, raise our corporate vision beyond
self-interest to the interests of our grandchildren who will inherit
the world we abuse. There's no plan B because there's no planet
B. May we hand on our precious planet in good shape, set on the
path to recovery. Help us to remember:

God saw everything that he had made, **and indeed, it was very
good.**

Ever-caring God, we thank you for those organizations that are
dedicated to the conservation and flourishing of our good earth
and its wildlife. We pray for them – the National Trust with its
swathes of moorland and coast, Friends of the Earth, the Council
for the Protection of Rural England, the RSPB and RSPCA,
A Rocha and many others. And especially we pray for the farmers
who do so much to sustain the beauty, diversity and productivity
of the land, and often get little thanks. Make us tender-hearted
and hard-headed so that, as a society, we care for our countryside
and its wildlife. Help us to remember:

God saw everything that he had made, **and indeed, it was very good.**

Ever-living God, teach us that the environment starts at our front door. Enable us to care for our immediate open spaces, our gardens and parks, our allotments and hanging baskets. May we leave streets without litter and public spaces without damage. We pray for council workers who maintain flower beds and strive to win awards. We pray for a sense of communal pride in making the most of our local environment. Help us to remember:

God saw everything that he had made, **and indeed, it was very good.**

Ever-creating, ever-sustaining and ever-living God, help us to share your joy in the beautiful miracle of planet earth. Make us co-creators of a renewed world that shines with your glory. Help us to remember:

God saw everything that he had made, **and indeed, it was very good.**

(55) PRAYER

Strangely, we don't often pray about prayer. But prayer is fundamental to our Christian living and deserves our prayerful concern. A possible verse and response would be: 'The disciples said, "Lord, teach us to pray."'

Loving God, you call us into closeness with you and yet we are strangely awkward about prayer. Help us to overcome our fear, reluctance and guilt, and give us the desire simply to spend time with you, relaxing in your presence, orientating our lives towards you.

The disciples said, 'Lord, teach us to pray.'

Loving God, thank you for implanting in us the instincts that lead to prayer. We can't help being thankful, or sorry, or full of wonder, or concerned for someone we know and love. All this is where prayer starts. Help us to trust our instincts and to stretch them out before you regularly, for in this way we'll deepen our relationship with you.

The disciples said, 'Lord, teach us to pray.'

Loving God, there are people we care about who have a variety of needs right now. To pray for them is the best way we can love them. So we pray for the people who are on our hearts – in pain, awaiting an operation, feeling depressed, struggling with an impossible situation. Here they are now, Lord, for you to touch with your life . . . *(space for people to pray silently)*.

The disciples said, 'Lord, teach us to pray.'

Loving God, make us a praying church, one that not only prays and values prayer but also teaches about prayer and loves to pray. Make us a kind church, not judging each other's spiritual maturity but simply acknowledging that we're all beginners in prayer, a body of seekers exploring spirituality together. And remind us how many people outside formal church life either do pray or want to pray. Make us helpful to anyone with whom we might share the journey.

The disciples said, '**Lord, teach us to pray.**'

Loving God, ultimately words are not enough; they crumble to dust in the heat of your presence – they feel so puny and inadequate. Draw us deeper into the stillness of your eternal presence so that we may know you, or know we have opened our lives to you, or know we have *wanted* to open our lives to you. Whichever it is, it is enough. Here we are, Lord, silently before you . . . *(longer silence)*.

The disciples said, '**Lord, teach us to pray.**'

And he did.

(56) SEEDS OF PRAYER

These intercessions develop the image of seeds in the hope that it will spark people's imagination and perhaps be an idea they could use in prayer at home. After each section leave a long enough pause for real prayer.

Jesus several times used the image of seeds to illustrate his teaching that small things have great potential, including small seeds of faith. Imagine, then, that in this time of intercession you're planting seeds of prayer in the garden of God's love laid out before you . . .

First of all, plant seeds of prayer for your family and close friends. These are the ones you care deeply about, knowing them well, with all their beauty and their sharp edges. You know their needs today, and their challenges. And you have such hopes for them. Plant those seeds of prayer for them now, and trust God to bring about the growth . . .

Now plant some seeds of prayer for people you know less well but who are part of the tapestry of your life. They may be people you work with or know through a charity or community group. They may be neighbours with whom you exchange cheerful greetings but not much more. Or perhaps people you see regularly at the shops or the school gate. See who comes to your mind. Plant seeds of prayer for these people whom you don't usually pray for, but whom God lays on your heart . . .

Now plant some seeds of prayer for people who are in the public eye, for good or ill. People in the news, political leaders under constant pressure, sportsmen and women with great expectations laid on them, celebrities with huge temptations to believe their own publicity. Who catches your eye? Who might be in particular need of support and wisdom at present? Plant seeds of prayer for some of these people now . . .

Further away in the garden of God's love, seeds of prayer are needed for places and nations collapsing under the pressures

118

of war or famine, natural disaster or bad government. Take a handful of seeds and plant them well, for this is where seeds get trampled on and birds eat them up. Plant those seeds deep and water them well, and be prepared to return often to care for the fragile early growth . . .

You have seeds left over. Cast them wide over the whole garden, for we have a world deeply in need of prayer at all points and all times. Cast those seeds with love and joy, for this is our privilege, to work with God to sustain and heal the world in anticipation of a new creation, a new Eden . . .

You have one seed left. At your feet is a special patch of soil where you can plant a seed of prayer for yourself. What does your heart seek? What do you most need? Where do you feel vulnerable? Plant that seed tenderly now . . .

Jesus said, 'If you have faith the size of a mustard seed you will say to this mountain, "Move from here to there", and it will move.' May it be so with these prayers, Lord, which we offer in Jesus' name.

(57) CHILDREN 1

A familiar response could be used.

Gracious God, those of us who have children are enormously grateful for the gift. Despite the heartaches there's huge fun and privilege in this responsibility, and a glimpse of both the joy and cost of your 'parenting' of humankind. Again this day we entrust our children to you, praying that all shall be well with them. Bless them, Lord; then bless them again.

Gracious God, children in our culture are under enormous pressure to conform and succeed, to be attractive, popular and cool. They have to grow up too fast and be wise too young. Give them courage to resist these pressures and to find their own path in their own time. Give them families, friends and role models who build up their confidence and self-belief. And whenever possible, give them faith in Jesus to be their rock, their guide and their inspiration.

Gracious God, we pray for our schools, that they may light a fire in our children that never goes out. For in our schools discoveries are made, aspirations raised and dreams nurtured. Or, sadly, discoveries are hidden, aspirations squashed and dreams repressed. So we pray for our headteachers, class teachers, support staff, governors, parents and all who are committed to excellence in education. Keep their standards high and hopeful, and their commitment at full stretch. And keep the well-being of the children themselves front and centre in all they do.

Gracious God, we pray for those of our children who have extra challenges to face as they learn about life and what they can do and be. We pray for those who have learning difficulties or long-term health issues, those with visual impairment or hearing problems, those whose families have fragmented or who have suffered sudden accidents, those who are bullied and, tragically, those who are abused. Loving God, surround these special children with both personal and professional support; give them

120

friends to listen to them, and your grace to overcome their challenges – these early entrants to your kingdom.

Gracious God, may your Church be a good home for all children – joyful, playful, wise and safe. Re-double our efforts to adapt our ways to the ways of the kingdom, for Jesus said that unless we accept the kingdom like a child we won't be able to enter it. May the Church be a community of grace for all humanity – with a little child at the door.

(58) CHILDREN 2

We all feel protective of children and want them to be free to flourish. The device used in these intercessions is to imagine that we are walking past photographs of children who represent for us entire groups of young people. It's important that the congregation be given sufficient time actually to pray for these children at the end of each bidding, so you may want to limit the number of biddings.

Jesus had a special care for children and wanted them to have easy access to him. We pray for children now by imagining we're walking through a gallery of photographs of children, taking time to pray by each one.

We stop first by a photograph of a child we know well in our family or among our friends, a child full of life, energy and mischief, packed full of potential, beaming at us from the photo. Pray, then, for this child and for others you know growing up surrounded by love and opportunity. Pray in the silence that follows that they may seize the day, every day, and grow to be full of kindness and wisdom . . .

We move on and stop next at a photograph of a child in a wheelchair. Her face is calm and determined, challenging us to take her seriously. Our prayers go out to all children who start their lives with a disability. Pray for them, that disability may not be a disadvantage but a different opportunity, that problems may be the birthplace of character and different kinds of success. But pray with compassion . . .

We move on and stop next at a photograph of a child in a war zone, face smeared with dust, eyes that have seen too much too young. There are great numbers of such children who have known fear and the death of loved ones from an early age. Pray for this child and for all his friends around the world, that they may yet know the redemptive power of love and the joy of peace . . .

We move on and stop next at a photograph we dread seeing: a child who's clearly very hungry, tummy swollen, stick-like limbs, eyes large and past understanding. The photograph sears your soul. It should not be like this. Pray for the aid agencies you support regularly, working ceaselessly to put poverty behind us and to make the world a more compassionate place. Pray for that child and all those like her . . .

We move on and stop next at a photograph of a child at school, head down over a piece of written work, engaging with the serious business of learning new things and gaining new skills. Pray for this child and the millions of children around the world who have restricted opportunities to go to school. Education and love are the two vital ingredients of a successful future, so pray for the children you know, and the ones you don't know . . .

Jesus said, 'Let the . . . children come to me and don't try to stop them, for it is to such as these that the kingdom of God belongs.'

(59) HOME

*The concept of 'home' is a powerful one for most people,
representing as it does security, love, comfort, relaxation and
much more. It's also a powerful concept in the Christian faith
which claims that our true and final home is in God. These
intercessions explore different aspects of this seminal image. A
familiar verse and response could be used.*

Ever-loving God, we thank you for the place we call home, where
we can throw off our coat, lay down our bag and know that
we can relax in warmth and security. We thank you too for the
relationships that make this place home, the loved ones who share
it or visit us here. Bless our homes, we pray; make them places of
peace, love and hospitality. And forgive us for sometimes messing
them up . . .

Ever-hopeful God, we pray for those who feel less confident about
the concept of home – those who find it difficult to meet mortgage
payments, and those who can't even get into the housing market.
Give them resilience and patience, and the help of family and
friends. Above all, help them never to lose hope.

Ever-compassionate God, we pray for the too-many people who
are simply homeless, who move from sofa to sofa, night shelter
to night shelter or, tragically, shop doorway to shop doorway.
Bless and strengthen the work of the many agencies involved with
homeless people, and make us a more compassionate society at
every level. And challenge us personally when we walk by on the
other side.

God of justice and mercy, millions of people have had to leave
their homes because of war, hunger and persecution. They drift
homeless across continents looking for somewhere to lay their
head, to start again, to have a life. Especially we pray at the
moment for refugees from . . . Please subvert our prejudices and
open our hearts so that all your children can be free and have a
place they can call home.

Ever-welcoming God, remind us that you are our true home
and we will be restless until we find our rest in you. Help us to
move beyond camping temporarily in your love and to move in
permanently, there to find lasting peace and joy, in the company
of Jesus Christ our Lord.

(60) COMMUNICATION

A possible verse and response would be: 'The Word was made flesh and dwelt among us.'

Loving God, human beings have never been so connected to each other. We communicate constantly through email, text messages, tweets, Instagram, Snapchat, mobile phone, Skype, WhatsApp *(or current favourites)*, and it's hard to know what to think. We can reach each other more than ever, but we can also avoid personal contact. Give us wisdom with our technology so that we remain in real, human contact with each other – and so that we don't misuse our technology by bullying or abusing others.

The Word was made flesh **and dwelt among us.**

Loving God, thank you for our news media, now using so many different platforms to keep us up to date. We pray for the journalists who handle these powerful tools of communication. Give them a sense of responsibility and pride in doing an honest and fair job. Enable them to sift genuine news from the hailstorm of rumour, gossip and fake news, and keep them true to the highest standards of journalism.

The Word was made flesh **and dwelt among us.**

Loving God, raise our eyes from our smartphones, laptops and tablets, and enable us to see each other not as items of information or portraits in our personal gallery, but as individuals made in your image and touched by your grace. Enable us to be attentive to each other, generous in time and in listening. So may we never rob anyone of their humanity but rather seek to build communities of friendship and care.

The Word was made flesh **and dwelt among us.**

Loving God, we pray for our communication as a church. Help us not to leave anyone out. Help us to use our website, emails, tweets and news-sheets *(as appropriate)* with sensitivity and care. And enable us to communicate something of the love we experience in Christ, so that others might be drawn into a community of acceptance and grace. *(Prayer for effective communication about particular events and programmes.)*

The Word was made flesh **and dwelt among us.**

Loving God, thank you for communicating with us in the only way we could grasp – a human life. Thank you for the Word made flesh and blood, for Jesus, the divine interpreter. May we live in him and he in us, so that by our words and our lives we may communicate the love, joy and peace that he gives and that the world so needs.

The Word was made flesh **and dwelt among us.**

(61) GIVING/STEWARDSHIP

These intercessions would fit into a service where the focus is on giving as part of a regular renewal of pledges or where the focus is on raising money for a special project. Care has to be taken because of the different financial positions of members of the congregation, and the prayers themselves must not harangue the people sitting innocently before us!

Ever-generous God, we thank you for the means we have to get by, the money that keeps the wolf from the door and provides us with good things. Thank you for the way that money keeps the world moving. Keep us, though, from greed, for when wealth becomes our goal it also becomes our god and it doesn't bring happiness. Keep us also from compromising with corruption in any form, even when we're told 'everyone does it'. For we know:

All things come from you, **and of your own do we give you.**

Ever-generous God, St Paul says you will always make us rich enough to be generous, and we remember the poignant example of the widow and the small coins she gave in the Temple. Enable us to experience the truth that if we give first there's always enough, but if we give last there's never enough. In our living and giving remind us that:

All things come from you, **and of your own do we give you.**

Ever-generous God, you know the needs of the church and the hope you have for us here. So often we think in terms of the scarcity of our resources when actually the problem is our abundance of resources – the people, the plant, the ideas, the goodwill, our own wealth, the gospel itself – none of which we fully use. Teach us the joy of giving – cheerful, positive, liberating giving – as we seek to echo your endless giving to us. Because:

All things come from you, **and of your own do we give you.**

Ever-generous God, we know the world to be a place of overwhelming inequality, where very few own so much and so many own so little. Work steadily through us all, we pray, to address what must, to you, look tragic. Break through the armour-plating of national self-interest so that we gladly accept the challenge and opportunity of the UN Sustainable Development Goals on poverty, hunger, health, education and climate change. Move us on from good ideas to good action, because:

All things come from you, **and of your own do we give you.**

Ever-generous God, it often seems that there's nothing money can't buy. But we know there is. Money can't buy courage, joy, forgiveness, faith that moves mountains, love that will not let us go. Thank you for the money we have. May we not envy what we don't have. Give us contentment, for:

All things come from you, **and of your own do we give you.**

(62) FAITH AND DOUBT

The priest or minister may hope that everyone before him or her on Sunday morning is a fully paid-up believer in all aspects of the Christian faith and has a vivid relationship with God, but this is obviously far from the truth. These intercessions try to be honest about the grey areas of our faith and to extend prayer from there.

Gracious God, we come to you not as 100 per cent believers without a shadow of doubt, but as honest seekers after truth, trusting that we are following the scent of eternity. We don't ask for the certainty that traps us in a padlocked box, but rather for the mix of faith and doubt that enables us to keep discovering more about you. May we never fear questions, for questions test the truth and give us a more secure place to stand.

Lord, we believe; **help our unbelief.**

Gracious God, when doubt has gone further, and we or others of our company have lost our way, when your voice has gone silent and the burning bush has gone out, give us patience to wait, to be still, to be open to friends, to knock gently on new doors, and to watch the dark horizon for cautious signs of dawn. Help us to understand that mystery can't be packaged and ordered online. Reassure us at a deep level that you are still God and we are still your people.

Lord, we believe; **help our unbelief.**

Gracious God, may our church be one that's open to the challenges of the world. May we not hide behind doctrine and liturgy and ecclesiastical correctness. Help us to meet people's search for something more in life, and to accompany them in their search for depth in a trivializing culture. Help us to identify those places where we can encounter the world's scepticism with grace and honesty, where we can listen without fear and share what we've found so far in our own journey.

Lord, we believe; **help our unbelief.**

Gracious God, we give thanks for a worldwide Church that's growing at an astonishing rate, and for men and women who demonstrate an inspiring faith in hard places. Give us, in our secular and post-secular West, the humility to learn our faith afresh and to embody that faith in new shapes of religion and religious life. May we discover how to pour the liquid gold of the gospel into new moulds, and so to continue holding out the Word of Life in a jaded culture.

Lord, we believe; **help our unbelief.**

Gracious God, we offer ourselves again to you, not as perfect Christians but as Christians in draft form, open to your encouragement and grace. Live in us, work in us, love through us, as we stumble hopefully through this week, seeking to follow your Son, Jesus Christ our Lord.

(63) TERRORISM

Terrorism has become established as a fact of twenty-first-century life, reaching into all corners of the world. These intercessions might be appropriate after a particular act of terrorism in the news, or at any other time, simply recognizing the world's anxiety.

Gracious God, acts of terror keep shattering the world's fragile calm. The word 'outrageous' doesn't even begin to cover it. We can't conceive of minds so damaged, and hearts so full of hate, that they would do this. And yet the indiscriminate destruction and maiming of innocent lives continues to rip through societies the world over. Patient God, may we not hide in despair, but rather take a deep breath and try again to orientate our world to the ways of peace.

Lord, bless the world, **and hear the cry of our hearts.**

Gracious God, we weep at the terrible damage done to innocent people shopping in a market, relaxing in a restaurant, walking to school, doing ordinary things, until their lives are changed for ever. Thank you for the heroic dedication of medical teams who have to start putting these broken lives back together, or have to tell distraught parents that there's nothing they can do for their precious children. We pray for these medics and for agencies such as MSF, for their fortitude, skill and compassion.

Lord, bless the world, **and hear the cry of our hearts.**

Gracious God, although evil has to be defeated, it first has to be understood. Give wisdom to the analysts of religious and political fundamentalism. Enhance the skill and proficiency of the security organizations; help them to gather intelligence, see round corners and anticipate acts of terror. Bring together the best minds we have to respond to these convulsions and to push back against terrorism. Give us also leaders of calibre and integrity to work together beyond the confines of nationalism. May this winter of the world be followed by spring.

Lord, bless the world, **and hear the cry of our hearts.**

Gracious God, when so much around us seems to drip with darkness, give us the humility to see that hatred has a cause and that it incubates in any human heart. The line between good and ill runs not *between* people but *through* us all. All have sinned and fall short of the glory of God. We stand before you ashamed at what we have done with the freedom you have given us and the world with which you have blessed us. Remind us, over and over, that we are made *by* love and *for* love, and that only *through* love does the world have a chance of moving forward. So deepen our love for this wounded world, and for one another.

Lord, bless the world, **and hear the cry of our hearts.**

(64) THE WORLD FROM SPACE

Only use this idea if you think the congregation would be comfortable imagining themselves looking at our planet from space, as in those photographs of some decades ago. A familiar response could be used.

In these intercessions please imagine that you're looking at our planet from space. Many of us can remember the first photographs of earth taken from a spacecraft, and the life-changing effect that had on the astronauts. See that view now: a beautiful, fragile ball of blue and white, brown and green, set against the blackness of space. Our planet, our home.

Creator God, thank you for this planet of ours with its incredibly complex life, its staggering beauty, its intellectual achievements, its artistic brilliance and social progress. Thank you for the way the earth is fine-tuned for life, and for the breath-taking detail of its evolutionary story. Make us ever more aware of the miracle you have entrusted to us, and the folly of the rampant greed that threatens the future of the planet. Make the issues around climate change our highest global priority – or else that fragile ball of blue and white will become dark for ever.

Creator God, as we look at this beautiful globe we don't see borders and battle lines, religions and rivalries, different coloured countries and age-old hatreds. We see a world of common causes and a single people we call humanity. Build up our confidence in a vision of peace, equality and human flourishing, so that war becomes a tragic relic of the past and reconciliation becomes the goal of every nation. We pray for our international institutions; may the United Nations indeed 'unite the nations' in the pursuit of a just sharing of all that the world offers.

Creator God, from space we cannot see – but only hear about – the movement of people across continents seeking safety and a better life. We hear of hard nationalism and fierce resistance to the plight of refugees and asylum seekers. But you have given us intellects, wisdom and compassion. Help us to use these gifts to find solutions that honour people's aspirations and promote common ownership of the planet.

Creator God, from space we cannot see the distinctions and prejudices around race, gender, religion and sexuality that scar our world. Help us to see as you see – only people, beloved, unique and gifted. May the blindness of our prejudice be replaced by a deep delight in human diversity. We praise you that we are fearfully and wonderfully made, each to the design of your love.

Creator God, thank you for this beautiful, fragile ball of blue and white, brown and green, set against the blackness of space. Our planet, our home.

(65) CIRCLES

*One danger with intercession is that it can seem to be
disconnected from our everyday lives. Praying for troublespots
and care for the elderly can seem worthy but remote. Prayer is
most vivid when it's about people close to us. These intercessions,
therefore, start with us in the middle and then spread out from
there. The main purpose is to give proper time for people to pray,
not to listen to us saying prayers on their behalf. Take it slowly
(and therefore you might need to limit the number of circles).*

In our relationships with others, we live in a series of concentric
circles, some people very close, others further away. In our
prayers now we're going to have a significant time to pray for
these different groups, to ask God's blessing on them. Please use
the times of silence to pray for the people who come to your
mind. If you're a visual person you might even like to see them
bathed in light, the blessing of God.

At the centre circle, alongside us, are the people with whom we
live day by day or, if we live alone, the people we see most often.
Who are they? What do they most need? Pray for God's blessing
on them today . . .

In the next circle are friends and members of our family whom
we feel close to even though we don't see them as often. Who
are they? What do we want for them? Pray for God's blessing on
them today. See them bathed in the light of that blessing . . .

In the next circle are members of this church, fellow members of
what St Paul beautifully called the body of Christ. Who's sitting
near you today? Whether you know them or not, pray for God's
blessing on them for this week . . .

In the next circle are people we see in our daily lives, our
neighbours, people at work or in our leisure groups, people we
speak to but don't know very well. Who comes to mind? Why
should they, also, not be bathed in the light of God's blessing?
Pray for them, for that blessing, that light . . .

136

In the next circle are people all over the country whom we once knew well, but now either they or we have moved away. But they still have a place in our hearts and memories. Who comes to mind? Where are they now? Pray for God's blessing on them and their lives . . .

In the farthest circle are people we know around the world: family, old friends, former colleagues, mission partners. Who comes to mind on this big map? Who is God nudging you to pray for, and what might they need? Pray for God's blessing on them now, God's light . . .

Gracious God, thank you for the many people who are special to us in our circles of relationship. Thank you for all they give or have given us, in love, friendship and shared experience. Cover them in your blessing today; never let them slip from your gracious hand. And keep us faithful in our praying for them, for Jesus' sake.

(66) MUSIC

There are several ways in which music can be integrated with intercession. A chant can be used between verses (Taizé's 'O Lord, hear my prayer' is common) and a verse of a hymn or chorus can be used to open and close a time of prayer ('Be still and know that I am God', 'Be still, for the presence of the Lord'). A good solo voice can be especially effective. However, music forms such an important part of our lives that it can be good to focus our prayers on the gift of music itself, in more conventional intercession.

Creative and loving God, we thank you for the way music moves and inspires us, not least in our worship. Thank you for those who lead our music in church, for their dedication and imagination, their musical gifts and desire to serve. May music take our worship higher and deeper so that we meet you in heart and mind, and are released to sing with joy.

Sing to the Lord a new song, **for he has done marvellous things.**

Creative and loving God, thank you for the hymn writers of old and the composers of contemporary music, for Charles Wesley and Isaac Watts, for Graham Kendrick and Stuart Townend. Thank you for the composers of great melodies, for Bach and Parry, John Bell and Matt Redman. *(You might need to choose your own musicians!)* Raise up, we pray, new generations of musicians to enable us to sing for joy in the company of your people, and to live our lives by the melody of your love.

Sing to the Lord a new song, **for he has done marvellous things.**

Creative and loving God, we pray for the impact of music on the many who come only occasionally to church but are open to the invitation of beauty and rhythm, of cadence and interval. May they encounter something of the harmony of your love and an echo of the angels' song of heaven, and so be encouraged to seek the Source of such glory.

Sing to the Lord a new song, **for he has done marvellous things.**

Creative and loving God, we confess that our lives so often fail to reflect the beauty and harmony of the music we enjoy in worship. We are sorry for the discord in our lives and the conflicts which occur in our communities. Move and shape us, we pray, according to the melodies of your peace and the grace of your presence, so that our lives and the lives of our churches offer you the praise and glory that is your due.

Sing to the Lord a new song, **for he has done marvellous things.**

These prayers we offer you in the name of the Great Conductor of the music of heaven, Jesus Christ our Lord.

(67) ONE PARTICULAR PERSON

I'm going to invite you to pray for five people today – five
people you choose for yourself. Only five, but they represent
many others. We often pray best when we have particular people
to pray for rather than a generality of people. And there'll be
substantial space for you to pray for each one.

First, please choose someone to pray for from your own family,
or a very close friend. You know this person well. He or she is
gifted, unique, loved by you and by God. You know this person's
strengths and needs, what they enjoy and what they fear. See that
person before you now in your mind's eye, and pray for whatever
God calls you to pray for . . . *(longish pause).*

Now think of a child you know well or reasonably well; the age
doesn't matter. See that child or young person in your mind's eye,
packed with potential but already shaped by the life chances their
upbringing gives them. You can see their emerging personality
and some of their gifts and preferences. What do you feel they
might need most at this stage of life? Pray for them now . . .
(longish pause).

Now think of someone in public life, a politician who carries
major responsibilities. You may only know him or her from a
distance but you have an opinion of that person. Who are you
choosing? Who comes to mind? You may or may not agree
with them politically but they have their needs too – of wisdom,
compassion, resilience, a home life, space to think and time to
laugh. Pray for that person in silence now . . . *(longish pause).*

Now think of someone whose health is a concern to them and to
you. You know something of their condition, maybe a lot. Who
are you choosing? How much do you know of their life history
and their health history too? How much do you know of the
treatment they're receiving and how hopeful it is? Whatever you
know, God knows more. Pray for that person, placing him or her
gently into the hands of God . . . *(longish pause).*

Finally think of someone who has died and who meant a lot to you. See that person in your mind's eye as you'd like to remember them. You remember the times you shared, the joy, the love, the learning. How did this person enrich your life? Take time now to be thankful for that person, and to commit him or her to the God who created and blessed them, and now holds them in eternal life . . . *(longish pause)*.

We have prayed for five people, but five who represent a world of special people, all loved by God. Lord, bless not just our five but a world of fives. Bless us, make us whole and finally bring us safely home, through the love of Jesus Christ our Lord.

(68) THE BEATITUDES

These prayers are more meditations than intercessions and can be used at any time because they come out of one of the core texts of the Christian faith. They work best with two voices, equally clear and preferably practised, so that timing, volume, emphases, etc., are understood. A pause for reflection needs to be left after each Beatitude.

Our intercessions are based on that provocative text, the Beatitudes. One way of entering the Beatitudes more fully is to see them as an encouragement to 'let go' of various behaviours that inhibit our lives. There will be a time for reflection between each Beatitude.

VOICE 1 Blessed are the poor in spirit . . .

VOICE 2 who let go of their need to be somebody special, to have status or recognition or celebrity . . .

VOICE 1 for theirs is the kingdom of heaven.

VOICE 1 Blessed are those who mourn . . .

VOICE 2 who learn how to let go of the pain of bereavement, inch by inch, drop by drop . . .

VOICE 1 for they shall be comforted.

VOICE 1 Blessed are the meek . . .

VOICE 2 who let go of the need to be right all the time, so hard in a self-assertive culture . . .

VOICE 1 for they will inherit the earth.

VOICE 1 Blessed are those who hunger and thirst for righteousness . . .

VOICE 2 who let go of their addiction to themselves and turn outwards to the needs of the world . . .

VOICE 1 for they will be filled.

VOICE 1 Blessed are the merciful . . .

VOICE 2 who let go of the age-old need for revenge . . .

VOICE 1 for they will receive mercy.

VOICE 1 Blessed are the pure in heart . . .

VOICE 2 who let go of the need to look good, but want to help others look good instead . . .

VOICE 1 for they shall see God.

VOICE 1 Blessed are the peacemakers . . .

VOICE 2 who let go of the need to win, but seek win–win solutions . . .

VOICE 1 for they will be called children of God.

VOICE 1 Blessed are those who are persecuted for righteousness' sake . . .

VOICE 2 who let go of a safety-first, no-risk approach to life and faith . . .

VOICE 1 for theirs is the kingdom of heaven.

God of blessing, thank you for showing us a different, better way: the way of love and letting go, taken to the limit on the cross and vindicated in the resurrection. Give us grace to attempt the same path of love and letting go, wherever that path may take us, for it will lead us finally to our home in heaven and the company of Jesus Christ, our Lord.

(69) AN ORDINARY SUNDAY

A familiar verse and response could be used.

Gracious God, this ordinary Sunday we gather today as your people, only a fraction of the community who live around us. We gather on their behalf, with the privilege of representing them before you, the One who unreservedly loves all people and sustains all things.

Look with mercy and love on those who are going out today to take the children to sport, to visit parents and grandparents, to keep up to date with friends, to catch up on the week's shopping, or simply to have lunch together and a day out. Bless the people of this *(village/town/local community)* as they pursue their dreams, fill their lives or just hope to get by. We pray especially for our neighbours and the people down our road, remembering them now in silent prayer . . .

This ordinary Sunday, look with mercy and love on those people who have to work today in our shops, hospitals, police, power companies, transport services, and those who have to work at home preparing for next week. We know we're deeply dependent on each other in a complex society. Bless those who are working on our behalf today, and give them rest and pleasure when their turn comes.

Look with mercy and love on our armed forces, always on duty to protect and support our freedoms. We commit to you our young people who train for danger, and our senior officers who are always thinking round the corner of the future to defend us from harm. Bless them and their loved ones, and keep us loyal to those who are loyal to us.

This ordinary Sunday, look with mercy and love on the poor of the world and those who are looking for a home, those who are ill in body or mind, and those who are struggling with life or with themselves. We call to mind particular people who are on our hearts . . . Jesus came that we should all have life in abundance;

bless those for whom that seems far away. Put in the way of each one of us this week someone we can help towards that abundance of life.

Look with mercy and love on us, gathered as your people on this ordinary Sunday. We each have our part to play in the body of Christ, this church. Help us to grasp again, on what seems like an ordinary Sunday, the great truth that the world is shot through with your presence, that nothing is foreign to you, that you are always there before us and that nothing, therefore, is really 'ordinary'. And in that confidence we offer you again all that we have, all that we are and all that we could be, as agents of your love this week.

(70) THE LORD'S PRAYER

This is the prayer we rattle off so often but rarely really think about. This intercession is an attempt to slow the prayer down and unpack it in such a way that we mean it. It works best if one voice says the familiar phrase and another voice prays the rest. It's not to be rushed.

Jesus' disciples asked him to teach them to pray and he gave them the prayer that's said millions of times a day throughout the world. But there's a difference between saying the prayer and praying it. So let us pray.

Our Father in heaven.

Thank you, Father, for letting us get this close; for letting us call you Abba, Dad. We're thrilled to be part of the family, with Jesus as our older brother. Make us more like him.

Hallowed be your name.

May your name be holy in a world that recognizes holiness in all the wrong things, worshipping money, sex, celebrity and power. Instead, may our vision be filled with the holiness of your beauty, tenderness and love.

Your kingdom come, your will be done, on earth as in heaven.

This is the most exciting prayer we could ever make, that your alternative way of living should be established here, among us, on earth, starting here and now. Help us, your Church, to be the test-bed of the kingdom, where we try out your commands and promises, and find them to be true.

Give us today our daily bread . . .

. . . so that everyone on earth has what they need to flourish and to enjoy life in abundance. We bring to your table the world's hungry outsiders and pray that finally, and together, we might come to the festival banquet where the last will be first and no one is forgotten.

Forgive us our sins as we forgive those who sin against us.

Help us to recognize our sin as addiction to ourselves, often at the expense of others. Then, Father, forgive, not with the easy tolerance of our age but with the rich, hard, shocking, life-changing forgiveness that we see coming from the cross. And give us grace to pass that forgiveness on to others.

Lead us not into temptation, but deliver us from evil.

Not just the little stuff, the failings and foibles to which we are all prone, but the heavy-duty, deep darkness that opposes your reign of justice and love all over the world. Help us to resist the massive attack of evil wherever we see it, including in ourselves, and to push back confidently in the name of Christ.

For the kingdom, the power and the glory are yours, now and for ever.

Thank you that the outcome of the struggle isn't in doubt. We can raise our eyes to the coming dawn because nothing can ultimately hold back your reign of love. In the resurrection nothing is left unchanged. Alleluia, alleluia, amen, amen.

7 INTERCESSIONS IN INFORMAL WORSHIP, SMALL GROUPS AND PRAYER STATIONS

BACKGROUND POINTS

The following ideas for intercession are run together because they could be applicable to any of the situations in the title, depending on the context. A small group in one church could be an informal service in another. Prayers usable in an informal service in one place might fit well as prayer stations in another. There's no need to be prescriptive. Here, though, are some background points:

- Remember that there are many forms of prayer. The ideas here are only about intercession. Other occasions for prayer might include thanksgiving, confession, praise, reflective silence, meditation on Scripture and so on. Make sure you know which kind of prayer you are trying to facilitate.

- Be certain that the type of prayer you envisage isn't just the latest idea (gimmick?) you've come across, but is really one that could help this group of people to engage with God. Think through who will probably be there and how they would manage with that form of prayer. Don't take people further than they will be comfortable going.

- The range of possible ways to pray and things to use is enormous, limited only by our imagination. Visit the website <www.pinterest.com> and click through to prayer stations and you'll be overwhelmed by the variety and creativity of the ideas offered. Go into a craft shop and you'll see loads of material that could spark off ideas for intercession.

- The secret of good intercessions of this kind is thorough preparation. You need to think through how you'll introduce the prayer and what words you'll use so that people can easily embark on the suggested method of praying. If you're using materials, you need to set everything up carefully beforehand and, in the case of prayer stations, have clear, brief, written instructions in large print on how to use this particular way of praying.

– In this preparation make the material you use and the presentation of it as good as you possibly can. The key qualities to aim for are simplicity and beauty. God deserves the best we can offer, and slapdash presentation suggests that we take God for granted. 'Worship' means 'giving God worth'.

– Don't rush. Many forms of intercession need time. It's usually the anxiety of the leader, not of the participants, that leads to inadequate time being left for the deeper engagement in prayer that we hope for. Trust people to find their own way, and trust God to be using the time available. God won't be getting impatient.

– Be sensitive to atmosphere. Try to sense how the particular experience of prayer is being received and adjust it if necessary, or quietly reiterate the way to use it. Listen to the heart of the occasion, your own heart and the corporate heart of the group.

– Respect privacy. If someone is still involved at a prayer station when the time of prayer is coming to an end don't insist he or she comes and sits down; there could be something important going on between that person and God. Equally, respecting privacy means not examining any written prayers left at a prayer station and trying to work out whose prayer it is afterwards.

THIS TIME TOMORROW (TTT)

Go round the group (or just ask a few of them), finding out what they will be doing at this time tomorrow. They might be at a meeting, at school, going to hospital, visiting a friend, being interviewed, helping at a food bank or any number of different activities. Then the leader, or preferably any of the people present, can pray for whoever is going to be in those particular situations, thus tying together the faith activity (informal worship, small group) and ordinary life. God is always present, and help is always available.

IN THE NEWS

Give out a number of newspapers and ask participants to look through them by themselves or with the person next to them, and see what strikes them as needing prayer. Tell people how long they have for this. After a while, gather up what is being said, perhaps asking for some of the news stories to be read out, and asking also what effect that story has on the person reading it. What follows can be open prayer or prayer offered by the leader.

WHAT HAS AFFECTED YOU MOST?

This way of praying allows both personal and world news to be the subject of prayer. It applies particularly to a small group setting where members are invited to share, briefly, the event or issue that has affected or moved them most in the last week. There should be no discussion of each event but rather a simple laying before each other of some significant experience or emotional response from the week. Having heard all that has been offered, the group then waits on God for three to five minutes, entering into those issues. Following this there can be open prayer or prayer by the leader, gathering up the often precious things that have been shared and giving them to God.

WORLD MAP OR LOCAL STREET PLAN

Spread out a map of the world with a good number of night-lights arrayed around the edges, together with one larger candle. Invite participants to take a night-light, light it from the

150

large candle and then place it on the map on a country that's undergoing difficult times, or where an election is coming up, or where there's a special connection with the church or the person praying. The night-light can be placed silently or with a short prayer. The leader will be ready to complement the lights with one or two more for places that might have been forgotten, and then says a rounding-off prayer.

A localized variation on this is to use a local street map and invite prayer for the various schools, businesses, council offices, churches, charities, banks, development plans, etc. Particular people can be prayed for, too, by placing night-lights on their street.

Small polished stones, both coloured and clear, are easily bought from craft shops or online and make a very satisfactory alternative to candles and night-lights.

CROSS AND CANDLES

A standing cross, large or small depending on the context, is placed in a visible position. A tall white candle is placed a distance away from the cross. Each person is given a night-light or a small candle. After an introduction, participants are invited to pray for any situation that's on their heart by coming forward, lighting their candle or night-light from the large white candle and placing it at the foot of the cross, either with a short spoken prayer or in silence. If candles are used rather than night-lights, a sand tray will be needed. Keeping the light low enables the night-lights and candles to glow attractively, and quiet background music may enhance the prayerful atmosphere.

NAILS

Each person is given a large nail. A cross is set up in the midst. The prayers might be focused on violence and terrorism around the world, on the oppression of minorities, or on the sins and failures of society at home. After an introduction on the purpose of the prayers, participants are invited to come forward and name the subject of the prayer as they place the nail at the foot of the cross. Clearly there are several variations on this usage. It can be especially vivid if people hammer the nail into the cross laid on the floor, but the effect can be disturbing and account should be taken of the sensibilities of the group. Rather than nails, sticky notes can be used and stuck to the cross if it's large enough, or luminous cards attached with tacky putty.

ELASTIC BANDS

Each person is given an elastic band. A discussion takes place about the tensions people experience in everyday life and the stress that many people live under. There are the tensions of work–life balance, being and doing, the sharing of responsibilities in the home, looking after different generations in the family, how money is spent and by whom, and so on. All the time the elastic bands will almost certainly have been stretched and pulled this way and that by the participants. After the discussion, prayers of intercession can follow, either led or in open prayer, depending on the nature of the event and the confidence of the participants. At a prayer station there is obviously no discussion. The elastic band can be taken away as a reminder and so that prayer can continue.

LEGO

The theme is reconciliation and the breaking down of barriers. A wall of building blocks is built beforehand, preferably using the larger bricks for younger children. If the context is a small group or informal worship, a discussion can take place about the barriers that exist between nations, cultures, religions, tribes, races, parts of society, families, rich and poor – whatever is most relevant or topical. Having identified the problems and noted the efforts going on by peacemakers and mediators, the opportunity comes to pray. Participants are invited to come forward and remove a brick from the wall, praying as they do so for a particular situation and the reconcilers in it. It would be good to see the wall completely broken through by the end.

WATER

Water is poured generously into the font, if in church, or a large bowl, if elsewhere. Around the edge are coloured or colourless stones. Invite participants to hold a stone as they identify the object of their prayer and then to place it carefully in the water, which here represents the enduring love of God. If the activity is being introduced verbally, the leader can refer to the way that water enhances the colour of the stones, and to the power of running water to smooth the most obdurate stones by its constant, inexhaustible action. God's love has extraordinary consequences.

DRINK OF WATER

The theme is the need in all of us for living water, the life of God within to sustain us. The introduction or discussion can be about what 'living water' really means and what difference the life of Christ within us can make. A large jug of water is surrounded by small plastic beakers so that each person can come up and pour some water from the jug and drink it slowly, reflecting on our need for the life of Christ to keep us spiritually hydrated. (We live in a spiritually dehydrated culture.) As intercession for another rather than prayer for ourselves, the drink is taken for that person who has need of the reassuring or healing presence of Christ. We pray for that person as we slowly drink the living water.

PRAYER TREE OR NET

Prayer trees come in a variety of forms. Some come in a pot as branches from the garden; some are beautifully made out of a variety of materials (mine is made of steel by retired shipbuilders in Sunderland); some are painted on walls. Intercessions are offered by writing on pieces of card which can be tied to the tree, or by ribbons tied there without words, or stuck to a wall. Such prayer trees can, of course, be left as permanent aids to prayer or used in worship for a focused time of intercession. Or again, the prayers can be taken out and offered at a particular service each week, or simply left in God's sight.

A variation on the tree is the net. This can be hung in some appropriate manner and place, and intercessions can be tied to the net or, if the mesh is the right size, prayers can be rolled up and placed in the holes of the net. There can be real pleasure in watching the net become ever fuller and more colourful as the prayers increase, knowing that God is working with those prayers in every situation represented there.

STRING OF BEADS

In parts of the Church there's a long tradition of rosaries and a more recent tradition of prayer bracelets. You need a basket of larger beads of many colours and designs. The practice of intercession lies in threading a number of beads carefully and prayerfully into a rosary or bracelet which can be worn, placed in a pocket or bag, or hung up in a visible place for regular or occasional use. Choosing and stringing the beads to represent places, situations or people is the heart of the intercession, together with continued use of the string of beads. What or who each bead represents needs to be remembered by the person who put the string together and therefore the number of beads needs to be realistic.

FOOD

Have two arrangements of food in the midst of the congregation or group. They represent extremes of eating habits between rich and poor, not only in the Global North and South, but also within most countries. One pile of food consists of some of the contents of a Western larder or fridge, the other the normal diet of a struggling family in a poor country. Research on the internet would suggest what foods should be displayed for the poorer family. In a service the intercession can be led; in a small group setting members themselves can pray. Some of the subjects could be:

- the inequality of diets, leading to obesity in some and malnourishment in others, even in the same country;

- the trade relationships between countries, protectionism and the fluctuating price of foodstuffs on the world market (don't tell God all the technical details!);

- small farmers who get exploited and lose their land;

- climate change leading to disastrous crop failures;

- the work of the aid agencies;

- government commitment to the UN's Sustainable Development Goals.

PLAYDOUGH

Playdough can be useful for a number of forms of prayer, e.g. self-offering and confession, but here we see its value in intercession. Everyone is given a piece of playdough or invited to take a piece of playdough at a prayer station. They can then shape the playdough to represent what or who they want to pray for. No words are used, so nothing is given away if the resulting shape is weird. However, the power of people's imagination almost unfailingly results in a valuable and quite different way of praying.

PLAYING CARDS

Playing cards can be used in a variety of ways but the important common factor lies in what each suit represents. In this form of prayer, *hearts* represent personal relationships and family life; *spades* represent working life and work issues; *diamonds* represent issues of wealth, poverty and inequality; and *clubs* represent community groups, charities and voluntary organizations.

155

One way of using the cards is to give everyone one or two cards and have them pray silently for people and places related to the suit's meaning. Alternatively, a single card can be dealt to each participant, and people are then asked to get into groups of the same suit to pray together. Or again, at a prayer station, a card of each suit can be laid out for people to pray for one or all subjects. Or the pack of cards can be placed, face down, and participants can then take the top card and pray for that suit's issues, afterwards placing the card face up on a separate pile. The variety of possible uses is clearly considerable.

WALKING PRAYER

One valuable form of prayer on the right occasion and with the right kind of weather is walking prayer. Participants are invited to go out for a 15-minute walk in which they ask God to go with them as they stroll around the neighbourhood, noticing people, places, situations, sights and sounds. They are invited to notice anything that particularly catches their attention and to ask, 'How is God present in this?' When participants have returned, the group can discuss what they've noticed and what the implications are for a world loved by God but often out of kilter with him. This can lead into intercession, although it may hopefully include thanksgiving as well. This exercise might appeal more to a younger than an older group, but it's possible to have a group go for a 'virtual walk', closing their eyes and going outside in their minds and memories, and again asking of what they see, 'How is God present here?'

LORD'S PRAYER

There is nothing more basic to Christian prayer than the prayer Jesus gave us, recorded at the beginning of Luke 11. The problem we have is our over-familiarity with it, and so anything that makes us go slowly and reach inside it is worthwhile. In terms of intercession there are at least two ways of using it. The first is for the leader to say it phrase by phrase, leaving space for participants to pray openly out of each one. Praying, 'your kingdom come . . .', for example, is a huge invitation with massive implications everywhere. To pray, 'give us today our daily bread . . .' leads us to pray for the daily needs of all of 'us', i.e. all God's children. Another way of praying the Lord's Prayer is to lead the prayer as above but simply keep between one and two minutes' silence after each phrase for personal prayer. On a retreat where we're saying the Lord's Prayer together regularly, I sometimes pause for one to two minutes after a different phrase each time we use the prayer, inviting people to pray that phrase meaningfully in relation to contemporary society or individual needs.

EXAMEN

A central part of Jesuit spirituality is the use of the examen, which is a way of reviewing the past day in the presence of God in order to learn from it and deepen our relationship with God. It's usually done individually but it can be done as a group and it then works like this.

First the group is told how the whole prayer process works so that there are no surprises and they can relax into it. Then they are invited to ask God for eyes to see the significance of what has happened in their lives over the last day or week.

Then comes the heart of the process. For ten minutes members of the group look over that last period (the day or the week) in order to see where they were most grateful or felt most alive or most engaged, connected, open to God, and also where they were most uncomfortable, negative or out of sorts, most blocked from the presence of God. The two phrases used by St Ignatius, the founder of the Jesuit Order, were 'consolation' and 'desolation'. What we are trying to do is to recognize how God was present, what God was saying to us, what God's call to us was and is now. It's a bit like running a film of our day and freeze-framing it at points of both positive and negative significance. At those places we spend time examining what was really going on.

After ten minutes the group discusses what members became aware of in that time of reflection, and there might be open prayer or prayer by the leader. The point of the exercise is deeper than just intercession, important as that is. In time we become more aware of the movement of the Spirit, more attuned to the presence of God in our lives, and this is the doorway into an altogether richer journey with God.

NIGHT PRAYER

One form or another of Night Prayer can round off a day or an evening meeting in a way few other forms of prayer can. It's not specifically an intercessory service, being more concerned to wrap the day up in God's secure presence, but it has opportunity for intercession and is included here for that reason. Night Prayer was known as Compline in the daily round of eight services ('offices') in monastic life. It has an other-worldly and reflective feel to it. The Church of England *Common Worship* Night Prayer is well established as a modern version of Compline,[1] but there are other forms of Night Prayer: the Evening Liturgy from the *Iona Community Worship Book*, for example, and Compline from the Northumbria Community's *Celtic Daily Prayer* (a different form for each evening).[2] Further afield, the *New Zealand Prayer Book* has an especially rich and satisfying version.[3] From the Episcopal Church in the USA, and now adapted for the United Kingdom in *Daily Prayer for All Seasons*, comes a different Compline for every season of the Church's year, among brief services modelled on all the monastic offices.[4]

AND FINALLY

As I hope has become clear, there are any number of starting points for intercessions in informal worship, small groups and prayer stations. It's a time to let our imaginations off the leash. You have to know your participants and what they can tolerate, but you can start almost anywhere. For example, with *shoes*. Raid your shoe, trainer, walking boot and slipper rack and have the collection suggest different sorts of people who need prayer. A *clock*, or our watches, can suggest prayer for people who always seem rushed and short of time, or for those for whom time is running out, etc. Holding *money* in our hands can suggest prayer for bankers, for those who have too little money and those who have too much; prayer too for the Chancellor of the Exchequer and the Governor of the Bank of England. Assorted *clean rubbish* can be used to suggest prayer about the extravagance and waste of our society, prayer about recycling and prayer for those who collect the rubbish from our doors.

You see the point? Prayer starts anywhere.

8 PERSONAL INTERCESSION

Much of our praying for others isn't in public worship or small groups; it's what we do on our own. We may have a daily framework of prayer or a loosely drawn way of praying. It may be that most of our praying is done 'on the run'. But in whatever way we do it, praying for family, friends, people in need or larger-scale issues is our own decision and choice. What follows in this section is a variety of ideas on how to do this in ways that will hopefully keep us faithful to this foundational Christian practice that's both our privilege and our responsibility.

Here, first, are some basic guidelines to set the context for personal prayer and intercession.

- Be comfortable that there's nothing odd about interceding for others. It's one of our most irresistible instincts. When we hear that someone we know is in trouble our hearts immediately go out to them. We want to help. We want to make a difference. For those of us with even the slightest instinct for the spiritual, we find that we're looking in the direction of God, whatever image of God we have.

- Praying for someone doesn't need permission, nor does it have a tight protocol to follow. We can pray immediately, anywhere, and in whatever words we like. Indeed, we don't have to use any words at all; it's sufficient to have those people and situations in our heart as we go to God. In a sense, prayer is an anarchic practice: there are no rules; we just place the person in God's hands, however we do it.

- Some of our praying, however, is likely to be done when we settle down at a special time to do so. At that point, the place is important. For some people it's vital to have a set place associated with prayer, e.g. a particular room or a corner of a room, a chair with a particular view, or a particular walk with the dog. Getting to that place already takes us halfway into prayer, so we're ready to pray

– rather than having to search out a place each time, which is distracting and off-putting. 'Know your place.'

- In our special place it can be useful to have things to hand which help us to pray: for example, a candle to light, an icon to focus on, music, a Bible and Bible-reading notes, a devotional book. You don't want to have to go and find such things each time you're ready to pray.

- It's valuable to have some buffer-space between whatever we've been doing before and this time of prayer. This is liminal space in which to cool down, an air-lock before entering sacred space. So it's good to keep a couple of minutes of quiet in which to begin directing our minds and hearts towards God. Relax the tensions in the body; breathe deeply, remember the presence of God. It might help to have a special phrase, verse or hymn with which to do this 'turning to God'. Ones that help me are: 'Be still and know that I am God', 'You, Lord, are in this place. Your presence fills it; your presence is peace', 'Before you, Lord'. Or it might be a verse of a hymn, like: 'Drop thy still dews of quietness till all our strivings cease. Take from our souls the strain and stress, and let our ordered lives confess the beauty of thy peace.' Or it might be a whole hymn; I sometimes use 'Be thou my vision'. Whichever way we choose, the mind is becoming still and focused. We're ready.

- Intercession usually takes place in the context of a wider practice of prayer. For some people the context will be regular Bible reading with notes to help and prayer to follow. For others it will be a form of 'daily office' from *Common Worship: Daily Prayer*, *Celtic Daily Prayer* or the many alternatives now available as the practice of having a framework for prayer grows in popularity. Or you can develop your own framework, using perhaps an opening prayer, a psalm, a Bible reading and prayers which include an offering of the day to God, and finish with

161

the Lord's Prayer. For others again it may not be regular
Bible reading or an office that helps but rather a time of
silence starting or ending with intercession. In any of these
contexts intercession is not the chief aim but is certainly an
important part.

BACK TO BASE

One of the simplest ways to organize our prayers, and one
to return to when we get a bit lost, is TCP – thanksgiving,
confession, petition. This takes us to the essential grid points of
prayer. There are always more things we are grateful for than
we have time to give to the practice – that's thanksgiving. We
know we always fall short of our best selves and need grace
to get up and keep trying – that's confession. And then there's
the opportunity to pray for others and for anything else in the
world – that's petition.

EXAMEN

The Jesuit examen was introduced in a group context in the
previous chapter. Here we see it in the way it has normally been
used, for the individual. The practice of the examen allows us to
look back at the last 24 hours and see where God has been both
more active and more hidden in our experience. Pared down and
simplified into four steps, it works like this:

1 We begin by asking God to bring to mind the things we
   should notice about the last day so that we can learn more
   about ourselves, and learn also to be more aware of God's
   presence.

2 Look back over the day to identify the times for which you
   are most grateful, or when you felt most alive, connected,
   upbeat. What was going on there? Why did you feel that
   way? What do you learn about yourself from that? What is
   God's call to you through that experience? It may have been
   a conversation with someone, the first time you heard some

music, something you read or saw that really excited you. Or it might have been something as simple as a child's smile or the sun slanting through a window. Sometimes there will have been a person involved in the experience, so you can pray for that person and whatever situation came with him or her.

3 Next, we look back through the day to see when we felt most disconnected, dulled down, out of touch, dissatisfied. Again, what was going on there, why did we feel like that and what do we learn from it? What is God showing us about ourselves? And who or what might we pray for in that situation, because something was amiss and, apart from whatever was going on in us, there might have been a burden someone was carrying or a situation that was seriously dysfunctional.

4 Last, we look at the day ahead as far as we know it, with the appointments we already have fixed, and we pray for God's good presence and peace at those times, and God's care for the people we're going to meet.

PRAY A PSALM

We may be used to praying out of a passage of the Bible but it can be valuable to spend time just with a psalm a day. All human life is there in the Psalms, including both the joyful and the bitter parts, and they encourage honest praying. At the start of the day we choose a Psalm, read it slowly and pray it. When we linger with a psalm we may find that we make all sorts of connections with people and situations we're involved with, and that can lead us to pray for them. We can return to the psalm at the end of the day too. We might not want to pray with some of the more lurid passages in the Psalms but even there we can pray for those who are trapped in hatred and the desire for revenge.

CIRCLING

The Celts had a particular way of praying that involved protecting people and places by circling them in God's care. They often prayed in the open air around high crosses and they would draw a circle with their outstretched arm around the village or house or family. David Adam's circling prayer is rightly popular.

> Circle me, Lord. Keep protection near and danger afar.
> Circle me, Lord. Keep hope within, keep doubt without.
> Circle me, Lord. Keep light near and darkness afar.
> Circle me, Lord. Keep peace within, keep evil out.[5]

We can circle our family, our home, our church, our community with the protecting love of God.

PHOTOGRAPHS

We can have photos of the people who are most special to us and pray for one a day, focusing on their life and needs and holding them in God's love. These photos can be kept together in a pile or an album in the place where we pray, or, these days, they could be on our mobile phone or tablet. Visual reinforcement can make a considerable difference to the reality of our praying, just as seeing photos of a disaster area on the television news makes our concern more real and more likely to lead to a practical response.

PRAYER BOWL

Write the names of people you want to remember to pray for on small cards and put them in a bowl. Every day you can take a couple of cards out of the bowl and carry them with you during the day, or put them on your desk or in a visible place in the kitchen. In a sense you're carrying them in your heart throughout the day. You can pray particularly for them when you take the cards out of the bowl and when you put them back that evening. You can put more people in the bowl at any time but might want to refresh it every so often, e.g. at the start of the month or of Lent and Advent.

HANDS AND FINGERS

We can use our hands to hold a family or group in our prayers. I often pray for the families of our two daughters, one family per hand, holding them firmly but tenderly before God. The physical action reinforces the mental and spiritual activity. Similarly, we can identify five people we feel particularly drawn to pray for and have each finger represent one person who is in our prayers and whom we take with us through the day. Sometimes simply seeing our hand might remind us of those five people and we name them again in our hearts before God.

HYMN OR SONG

Hymns and contemporary songs are a fertile source of inspiration for prayer. We all have our favourites, and we can make sure we've learnt a few by heart and use them when we pray: for example, 'Dear Lord and Father of mankind', 'When I survey the wondrous cross', 'All I once held dear'. Obviously many hymns have personal devotion as their main focus but when we ponder a hymn deeply, other connections can come to mind and we can find there are plenty of people to pray for. Try it with your favourite hymn . . .

WALKING

The rhythm of walking may be conducive to prayer. In my experience it's more a time to chat somewhat randomly with God rather than to pray intensely for people, but we might want to 'take someone for a walk with us', in our heart. While walking we're bound to see people and situations deserving of our prayerful concern too. We see someone struggling with children, shopping and a buggy; we see someone having difficulty walking; we see a shop that's closed and with it perhaps someone's dream;

we see a group of teenagers, an Oxfam shop, a notice about a dementia group, and so on. Here are people and issues of real concern, all of which can be the subject of prayer. It makes walking to the shops much more interesting.

USE OF THE BODY

Not everyone will be drawn to this way of praying, but the body has been used in prayer for centuries. Think of David dancing before the Ark of the Lord, or Jews rocking back and forth at the Wailing Wall, or Shakers in the United States, Roman Catholic priests prostrating themselves at their ordination, charismatic worshippers in full flow. In simpler ways we might find using the body helpful in aligning our whole selves with the intention of our hearts. So, for example, it may be beneficial in prayer simply to *open our hands on our knees* as an act of opening ourselves up to God, ready to receive. Many people hold their hands out in front of them, palms up, when saying the Lord's Prayer in worship because it seems to express the openness they want before God.

We can hold someone before us in our open hands and then *bring our hands up to our heart* to express our 'heart-felt' intercession for them. When praying about some terrible occurrence we might *cover our eyes with our hands*, then slowly *lower our hands and separate them* as we pray for God to bring help and healing to those involved. When praying for someone in pain we might *wrap our arms around our middle and bend slightly forward*, as pain sometimes leads us to do. We might then find we identify more with the sufferer as we pray. If we're praying for ourselves and wanting to be totally available to God we might *reach our arms upwards in the shape of a chalice*, asking God to fill us with grace. The body is there to help. We don't live *in* a body; we *are* a body.

TRIGGERS

If we are interceding through the day, praying 'on the run', there will be many things we come across that can trigger our praying for others. The *sound of ambulances or police cars* chasing off to an incident gives us the opportunity to pray for whatever and whoever it is that they are going to. We don't then feel helpless but can co-operate with the help that's on its way. Again, as above, whenever we see *people in the street* whose predicament particularly moves us we can offer God's love and compassion in both prayer and action.

When we *run water from the tap* we could pray for those millions for whom that's a dream. When *queueing in a supermarket* we can pray for those who spend their lives at the back of the queue, longing for the things we take for granted, or those who are waiting for an operation, or a job, or someone to love them. When we *pass a prison* there are people in there; when we *pass a bank* there are big issues around our financial system; when we *pass a school* there are people's precious children there, and dedicated teachers and volunteer governors. All triggers to pray.

Another set of trigger opportunities for prayer exists as we communicate with each other. When we *sign a letter, end a phone call, text someone or email them*, there's a person at the other end of that communication and we could pause for a moment and add a prayer for their well-being. It doesn't take a moment; God doesn't need a particular quantum of time, just the opening.

LORD'S PRAYER

As we saw in the previous chapter, the Lord's Prayer is the model prayer on which we can hang all sorts of prayerful activity. We can pray it slowly, pausing between each phrase, or pausing especially at one phrase each time and lingering over what it really means and what we can pray for out of it. 'Deliver us from evil' enables us to pray for what strikes us as evil in the state of the world at present, just as 'lead us not into temptation' (or 'the time of trial') can lead us to pray for the host of temptations that old and young are prey to in today's libertarian culture. We could take 'a phrase for the day' and see where it resonates with what happens during the day, praying as we go. We could make praying the Lord's Prayer the focus of an entire quiet day – no more might be needed. It is, after all, the prayer our Lord himself gave us.

9 INTERCESSION FOR EXTROVERTS

When it comes to personal prayer it has to be admitted that most advice seems to come from introverts. It's introverts who seem to write most of the books on prayer and lead the retreats and quiet days. The good news is that prayer is for extroverts too – and for hard-pressed parents who have young children around them all the time and are left with little space for reflection and prayer. So here are some ideas that might help.

ENJOY LIFE!

In other words, relax and get on with living life to the full in the light of the God who is always present. After all, God isn't so much interested in whether we are wonderfully religious as whether we are fully alive. God is the Source and Ground of everything and the 'Inwardness' of everything that exists, every quark and meson, every star and galaxy, and we have the wonderful opportunity of exploring this 'everything'. The rabbis used to say that the first question we would be asked by God at the end of life would be, 'Did you enjoy my creation?' As we enjoy life we can chat with God as we go, responding to the reminders of God's presence and the needs of people around us. This 'practising the presence of God' is a lovely background to a busy life, remembering and smiling in the direction of God and putting others into God's care. So, enjoy life and remember God.

WALKING AND RUNNING

For many extroverts and busy parents one of the times to pray can be when out walking and being stimulated by the sights and sounds around them. Extroverts are typically energized by the outside world, so walking (or going out for a run) may be a good time to pray over things both around you and in your mind. Issues can arise and get sorted with God in the context of the steady rhythm of walking and running. On the other hand, if you are out with two children, a buggy and several bags of shopping this may not work . . .

JOURNEYS

Another time that can be well used for prayer is the enforced inactivity of being in a car or on a train going to work. The outside stimulus is still there, and as it's a necessary pause in the day, why not pray? It can even be a time to use a daily office on a phone app (though not while driving!). There's great value in setting the day in the context of God early on; soon enough it will be filled with demands, so let's get the 'direction' of the day sorted out at the start. The purpose of prayer is that we should live our lives in the direction of God.

GARDENING

On the other hand, if you are home-based, I have it on good authority (my wife) that gardening is a very good time to pray. You are focused and uninterrupted. Your mind can go free, relatively speaking, while your hands do the work. Having those hands deep in the soil is another benefit; it reminds us of our earthy origins. (Adam came from the *adamah*, Hebrew for earth.) The rhythm of grass-cutting is another opportunity to pray, surrounded by the realities of God's 'other book', the natural world.

PRAYING WITH OTHERS

Extroverts are more likely to pray when in the company of others and stimulated by their presence. This means that prayer is easier in public worship or in a group than by oneself. The group may be a home group meeting fortnightly or a prayer triplet meeting over coffee or before work, but in whatever way we meet, the benefit of sharing prayer with others goes to the heart of the corporate nature of faith. We are meant to be together. The

Church is a body with many members (1 Corinthians 12.12), so groups both large and small, Sunday or midweek, are very much a natural context for prayer.

KINGDOM-BUILDING

Perhaps it helps to see that work can also be understood as prayer. The monastic tag was *laborare est orare*, to work is to pray. As we work constructively and conscientiously we are making another tiny contribution to building the kingdom of God, the flourishing of all things. This may be more obvious when we are engaged in some overt action for social justice or the transformation of that bit of creation in which we are set, but all work done in harmony with God's good purposes for the world can be seen as an offering to God. And that's what prayer is – offering ourselves, others and the world to God. Extroverts in particular can be liberated by this kind of approach to work and prayer, but it applies to us all.

RETREATS

Strange as it may seem, extroverts are often much helped by going on retreat and keeping quiet. The psychoanalyst Carl Jung would explain it by saying that we all need to 'round out' our preferred personality type by drawing on our opposite type, part of a process he called 'individuation' whereby we come to a mature and integrated wholeness. As extroverts usually get their energy from outside themselves, they sometimes need to replenish from the inside as well. This is what retreats and quiet days can offer. It means that the extrovert gets focused, quality time with God and can live on the fat of the spiritual land (as it were) for quite a time afterwards.

COLOURING!

Another unlikely occupation which can help some people to pray is the recent resurgence in the practice of colouring. There has

171

been a flurry of books offering the opportunity for people of all ages to colour-in various designs as a form of calming, reflective activity. For Christians this seems to be somewhere in the contemplative register. The subject may or may not be spiritual (though there are books specifically produced by Christian publishers) but the activity in itself involves concentrating on the present moment, which is at the heart of prayer, and producing something of beauty, which is a common Christian calling. It might be worth a try.

NOTES

1 Night Prayer from *Common Worship: Daily Prayer* (London: Church House Publishing, 2005).

2 The Northumbria Community, *Celtic Daily Prayer* (London: HarperCollins, 2015).

3 The Anglican Church in Aotearoa, New Zealand and Polynesia, *A New Zealand Prayer Book* (Christchurch, New Zealand: Genesis, 1989).

4 John Pritchard, *Daily Prayer for All Seasons* (Norwich: Canterbury Press, 2016).

5 David Adam, *The Edge of Glory* (London: SPCK, 1985), p. 8.

FURTHER RESOURCES

David Adam, *Prayers of Intercession* (Stowmarket: Kevin Mayhew, 2012).

Ian Black, *Intercessions for Years A, B and C* (London: SPCK, 2009).

Doug Chaplin, *Leading Common Worship Intercessions* (London: Church House Publishing, 2015).

Raymond Chapman, *The Intercessor's Guide* (Norwich: Canterbury Press, 2007).

Raymond Chapman, *Leading Intercessions: Prayers for Sundays, Holy Days, Festivals and Special Services Years A, B and C* (Norwich: Canterbury Press, 2014).

Simon Pothen, *Intercessions for Daily Prayer* (Norwich: Canterbury Press, 2009).

John Pritchard, *The Intercessions Handbook* (London: SPCK, 1997).

John Pritchard, *The Second Intercessions Handbook* (London: SPCK, 2004).

Susan Sayers, *Prayers of Intercession for Common Worship* (Stowmarket: Kevin Mayhew, 1999).

Compilation books of prayers, including intercessions

Angela Ashwin, *The Book of a Thousand Prayers* (London: HarperCollins, 1996)

The SPCK Book of Christian Prayer (London: SPCK, 1995)

Flo's Story

A little story about prayer

After I was widowed, my daughter Jo persuaded me to go to this tea dance in a church hall, a bus ride away from where I live. It was a way to keep fit and meet a few people and really cheered me up, but I still felt empty inside.

One day Dot, the lady who runs the dances, was handing out these little *Prayers on the Move* booklets, so I took one. I hadn't been to church for years and I hadn't prayed for a long time, but reading this little book, by myself, in my own time, the prayers really spoke to me. I realized what had been missing.

The next week, I told Dot that I'd really enjoyed the book and said I thought it would be nice to go to church. Dot said she'd give me a lift. Now I'm going to church every Sunday, I've found my faith again and I'm so happy. That empty feeling inside has gone away and it's all thanks to a little booklet called *Prayers on the Move.*

Inspired by a true story. Names and places have been changed.

Help us to tell more stories like Flo's. Sign up for the newsletter, buy bags, books and travelcard wallets, and make a donation to help more people like Flo find God through a book. www.prayersonthemove.com.